Also available at all good book stores

9781785319792

9781785318832

9781785316470

9781785318221

9781785319938

9781785311987

9781909178731

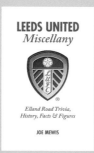

9781905411962

9781905411535

LEEDS UNITED

MINUTE BY MINUTE

LEEDS UNITED
MINUTE
BY MINUTE

Covering More Than 500 Goals,
Penalties, Red Cards and
Other Intriguing Facts

DAVID JACKSON

First published by Pitch Publishing, 2021

Pitch Publishing
A2 Yeoman Gate
Yeoman Way
Worthing
Sussex
BN13 3QZ
www.pitchpublishing.co.uk
info@pitchpublishing.co.uk

© 2021, David Jackson

ISBN 978 1 78531 978 5

Typesetting and origination by Pitch Publishing
Printed and bound in Great Britain by TJ Books, Padstow

Contents

Extra time

To Brenda and Ron
Turner, Kim and Malcolm
Hogan, and Deb and Nick
Kermode. Thank you.

Acknowledgements

Leeds United: Minute by Minute was a hard book to research, with many hours spent watching goal after goal, trying to figure out who set them up, and many more hours searching for details in old newspaper clippings and match reports.

Grainy footage, unclear commentary or odd angles can make the task that much harder, but thanks to certain resource outlets the task became a lot easier.

The goal times are taken from various resources, including BBC match reports, Sky Sports games, *Match of the Day*, endless YouTube highlights, plus Leeds United FC's official website and various other fan sites and stats platforms such as Opta, Soccerbase, Transfermarkt and 11v11.

But a couple of websites in particular proved goldmines of information, with goal times and match reports that would otherwise have been lost in the passage of time. With that in mind, I must firstly thank Dave Tomlinson and his Mighty Leeds website. I'm certain all United fans will be well aware of Dave's work and his books, but if somehow they have passed you by, please visit www.mightyleeds.co.uk. Being able to cross-reference old YouTube clips with match reports is vital in writing a book like this and Dave's goldmine of stats, results, reports and memorable moments helped me fill in a lot of gaps.

The same could be said of Tony Hill's excellent Oz White website, which again gave me vital info, stats and facts that were almost impossible to find elsewhere. The site can be found at www.ozwhitelufc.net.au and again, if you've not visited as yet, make sure you do because you won't be disappointed.

As a writer, I like to be as honest as possible and so will admit to not being a diehard Leeds United fan – I hope that sits okay with everyone. I've always had a soft spot for Leeds over the years and I first saw them play in the late 1970s, when, as a small kid, I watched Joe Jordan and Gordon McQueen inspire (or bully) a victory over the side I supported at our home stadium. I walked home in awe with my older brother. 'You've just witnessed two of the best headers of a ball in this country,' he told me. I never forgot that and I loved the Admiral white with yellow and blue piping strip that Leeds side wore – I still do, if truth be told.

ACKNOWLEDGEMENTS

A few weeks later, I remember seeing on the back page of our local paper – if memory serves – that both Jordan and McQueen had joined Manchester United for a combined fee of £500,000. If I say I wasn't best pleased, at least it will hopefully reassure readers that my loyalties most certainly don't lie at Old Trafford!

Finally, I'd like to say a massive thank you to Paul and Jane Camillin – the tireless siblings who mastermind Pitch Publishing – for commissioning this series of *Minute by Minute* books. And thanks to both for their patience as endless deadlines passed silently without complaint.

Introduction

Leeds United Football Club have an extraordinary record and *Leeds United: Minute by Minute* takes you through the Whites' matchday history, recalling the historic goals, incidents, sendings-off, penalty shoot-outs and other memorable moments, all catalogued by the minutes they happened in.

You'll be able to rememeber some of the club's most iconic matches or simply relive some truly unforgettable moments from Leeds' glorious past, from the magnificent Don Revie era and the United greats who formed a team that was feared and revered in equal measure for a decade in this country through the Howard Wilkinson years and on to the present and the sparkling football played under Marcelo Bielsa.

Goals from Eric Cantona, Mark Viduka, Mick Jones, Allan Clarke, Tony Yeboah (what a player he was, with a shot like a thunderbolt), the great Peter Lorimer, Eddie Gray and a cast of hundreds are recounted in detail, with the brilliance of Billy Bremner, the grit and determination of Jack Charlton and Norman Hunter or the guile and finesse of the brilliant Johnny Giles sprinkled liberally throughout.

But there is also the odd name here and there that may have been lost over the years, plus rare efforts from the likes of Gary Kelly and Danny Mills – and even at least a couple from Luke Ayling.

Added to these great names are dramatic winners in FA Cup and League Cup ties, Europe, play-offs, title deciders and matches played from the Camp Nou and Wembley to Vale Park and Wimbledon.

Volleys, tap-ins, long-range efforts, free kicks, own goals and penalties – not to mention those moments of madness and controversy – plus the occasional painful strike against the Whites; it's all remembered with vivid descriptions that should bring back mostly happy memories for all United fans.

Plus – and fascinatingly – you will also discover just how many times a crucial goal has been scored at the same minute so often over the years, from goals scored in the opening few seconds to the last-gasp extra-time winners that have thrilled generations of fans at Elland Road and around the world.

One thing I learned with some certainty – and that is apart from the undoubted highs there have been – is that being a Leeds United fan brings with it a lot of heartache and, though I believed I knew plenty about the club, I was amazed to discover how many near-misses the Whites have endured, particularly in the 1960s and 1970s. And, for want of a better word, it's hard to believe a club could be cheated out of two major European trophies in the way Leeds United were. Enough said.

Now, on with the show. Enjoy, relive and recall.

Minute by Minute

First half

10 seconds

3 November 2004
Leeds United v Burnley, Championship

The fastest goal in the Whites' history comes against Burnley at Elland Road. The game has literally just kicked off when Matthew Kilgallon plays a hopeful ball forward and Brian Deane flicks it on to David Healy who cushions it for Jermaine Wright to make no mistake from close range and put United 1-0 up. The Clarets recover to win 2-1, but Wright at least wrote his name into the record books with the quickest Leeds strike on record. At the time of writing, Wright is still the proud holder of this unique stat.

11 seconds

17 March 2001
Charlton Athletic v Leeds United, Premier League

Mark Viduka puts the Whites ahead at Charlton with what at the time is the club's all-time fastest goal, and the second-fastest in the Premier League at that point too. The goal comes when David Batty plays a pass to Ian Harte, who hoofs a speculative ball forward. Alan Smith manages to flick it into the path of Viduka, who takes one touch before firing past Addicks keeper Saša Ilić to give the Whites a flying start.

12 seconds

12 January 2016
Ipswich Town v Leeds United, Championship

Souleymane Doukara takes just 12 seconds to give United the lead at Portman Road. When a long ball is played towards the Ipswich defence, it is headed across the edge of his own box by a home defender and as a team-mate collects in the middle, Doukara steals the ball and then lashes a low shot into the bottom-right corner to put Leeds 1-0 up. Brett Pitman will score in added time to give the Tractor Boys a 2-1 win to make it a miserable Tuesday evening in Suffolk.

16 seconds

1 March 2019
Leeds United v West Bromwich Albion, Championship

Pablo Hernández scores to leave West Brom reeling in a Championship promotion clash at Elland Road. Marcelo Bielsa's men, fresh from a 1-0 loss at QPR, race out of the blocks at Elland Road and go ahead in stunning style as Hernández sets the Whites on the way to a thumping 4-0 win over Darren Moore's men – and the Baggies had kicked off. Jack Harrison wins possession and races down the left flank before spotting Hernández in acres of space outside the West Brom box – he passes to the Spaniard who takes a touch before rifling a superb shot into the top-left corner from 20 yards to send Elland Road wild.

20 seconds

21 January 1984
Leeds United v Fulham, Second Division

It's rare that a winning goal comes just 20 second into a game, but that's what happens when Leeds host Fulham in the second-tier at Elland Road. Andy Watson is the hero, catching the Cottagers cold from close range to give Eddie Gray's struggling side a 1-0 win in an otherwise largely forgettable game.

35 seconds

17 September 1969
Leeds United v Lyn, European Cup first round, first leg

League champions Leeds make a stunning European Cup debut against Norwegian champions Lyn in the first leg at Elland Road. United take the lead with the first attack of the game as Paul Madeley's superb precision pass finds Mike O'Grady's run as he cuts inside on the left of the box and he then hits a thundering a angled, rising shot past the Oslo side's keeper and into the far right of the net.

2

28 December 2009
Stockport County v Leeds United, League One

Runaway leaders Leeds get off to the perfect start at Edgeley Park against bottom-of-the-table Stockport County. The hosts, who have suffered ten successive defeats, couldn't have made a much worse start as Robert Snodgrass takes the ball towards the box before unleashing a left-foot shot that dips over the keeper and into the top-left corner to give Simon Grayson's men a 1-0 lead on a mud bath of a pitch.

3

12 September 1995
AS Monaco v Leeds United, UEFA Cup first round, first leg

United are gifted a vital early away goal against Monaco after a dreadful defensive mix-up. Tony Dorigo sends a hopeful cross into the Monaco box towards Tony Yeboah, but the keeper and central defender both go for the same ball and get in each other's way. The loose ball falls to Yeboah who doesn't wait for a second invitation as he sends a sideways bicycle kick into the unguarded net to put the Whites 1-0 up.

12 August 2008
Chester City v Leeds United, League Cup first round

Jermaine Beckford's predatory instincts are at their best as he gives United an early lead away to League Two Chester City. There is a rare assist for United keeper Casper Ankergren, too, as the Dane sweeps a 60-yard pass towards the Chester six-yard box and Beckford is alive to the opportunity as he slides in ahead of a defender and the keeper to divert the ball into the bottom-right corner and put the Whites on the way to a resounding 5-2 victory.

8 February 2021
Leeds United v Crystal Palace, Premier League

Jack Harrison's first season as a Premier League player just gets better and better as he scores another fine goal to put the Whites 1-0 up against Crystal Palace at Elland

Road. The opener comes when Stuart Dallas plays a short pass to Harrison just outside the Palace box — with no immediate challenge, the on-loan Manchester City man nudges it into the box before unleashing a powerful rising shot that gives the keeper no chance as it flies into the roof of the net to put Leeds 1-0 up. Stunning stuff from a player who only seems to score spectacular goals.

4

17 September 1969
Leeds United v Lyn, European Cup first round, first leg

United double their lead against Lyn with another excellent goal. The first goal had come via a move down the left flank and the second comes from the right as Paul Reaney sends in a perfect cross that Mick Jones leaps up for and heads across the keeper and into the top-right corner to make it 2-0 in no time at all as the Norwegian part-timers buckle in for a long evening.

16 May 1973
Leeds United v AC Milan, European Cup Winners' Cup Final

On a heartbreaking and controversial night at the Kaftanzoglio Stadium in Thessaloniki, AC Milan grab the only goal of the game to end yet another trophy dream for an injury- and suspension-hit Leeds side who had looked on course for a league, FA Cup and European treble at one stage. Worse still, there are accusations levelled against referee Christos Michas, who continually appears to favour the Italians with any borderline decisions and will later deny the Whites at least one clear-cut penalty in the first half. For the winning goal, the free kick awarded on the edge of the Leeds box is questionable to say the least and Luciano Chiarugi's low shot takes a slight deflection off Paul Madeley and flies in off the foot of the right post and into the net. The Greek referee will eventually be banned for life for match-fixing, though allegations that he had been bribed ahead of this match will never be proved.

25 September 2012
Leeds United v Everton, League Cup third round

The Whites get off to a fantastic start against Premier League Everton with a goal inside four minutes. The Toffees, second in the top flight, are strong favourites against Neil Warnock's side, but an early misplaced pass in defence allows Leeds in for the opener as Rodolph Austin's challenge allows Aidy White to burst towards goal and as two Everton defenders race to close him down, his rising shot beats the keeper to give United a 1-0 lead at Elland Road.

5 December 2020
Chelsea v Leeds United, Premier League

Patrick Bamford gets United off to a dream start away to Chelsea with a goal after only three minutes at Stamford Bridge. Kalvin Phillips looks like he is out of options on the left of the halfway line, but he spots Bamford's run down the middle and plays a perfectly weighted ball into his path. Bamford nips in between Kurt Zouma and Édouard Mendy, taking the ball past the French keeper and then slotting into the empty net to make it 1-0. It is especially sweet for Bamford who had spent five years with Chelsea without ever making a senior start, but despite the bright beginning, the hosts will battle back to win 3-1.

5

7 October 1967
Leeds United v Chelsea, First Division

Leeds, beaten in the FA Cup semi-final by Chelsea just five months previously, are thirsty for revenge against the west Londoners. And with Chelsea manager Tommy Docherty resigning the day before, the visitors are clearly still shaken from the events of the past 24 hours – even more so with the thrashing they will receive from Don Revie's side which begins when Billy Bremner's clever pass finds Paul Reaney who crosses in for Albert Johanneson to head home the first of the afternoon.

24 October 2000
Leeds United v Barcelona, Champions League first group stage

Having lost the first group meeting 4-0 at the Camp Nou, United look to avenge that at Elland Road and are given the ideal basis to do so through Lee Bowyer's excellent fifth-minute goal. Abelardo Fernández's foul on Mark Viduka on the left allows Bowyer just enough sight of the Barcelona goal and his curling free kick escapes the grasp of keeper Richard Dutruel as it bends into the top-right-hand corner of the net to make it 1-0.

4 May 2003
Arsenal v Leeds United, Premier League

United's hopes of surviving relegation get an early boost at Highbury through a Harry Kewell goal. With Peter Reid in temporary control of the Whites, the second-placed Gunners strike the woodwork through Martin Keown in the opening moments, but Leeds catch the hosts cold with a counter-attack as Jason Wilcox plays a long ball forward into the path of Kewell who races on to the pass before sending a ferocious left-footed, angled drive across David Seaman and into the net from 20 yards out – a stunning strike from the livewire Aussie.

11 August 2018
Derby County v Leeds United, Championship
United grab an early advantage at Pride Park with a goal in the first attack of any note. Both sides have started their campaign with a victory and are keen to lay down a marker, but it is United who silence the home support when Samuel Sáiz plays the ball infield from the left flank to Pablo Hernández, who in turn rolls it sideways to Mateusz Klich who skips past one challenge before rifling a powerful shot into the corner to make it 1-0.

19 September 2020
Leeds United v Fulham, Premier League
In United's first home game since winning promotion back to the Premier League, Hélder Costa spectacularly opens the scoring against Fulham. The match, played behind closed doors at Elland Road due to the Covid-19 pandemic, explodes into life when a deep corner is nodded backwards by a Fulham defender to Costa on the left corner of the six-yard box and after controlling the ball, he fires a shot in off the underside of the crossbar and into the net to make it 1-0.

27 December 2020
Leeds United v Burnley, Premier League

United get the early breakthrough against Burnley with a goal that will settle the contest just five minutes in. Patrick Bamford is alive to a long ball played towards the Burnley box and as he brings it under control, he takes it away from England keeper Nick Pope and is clattered in the process by the Clarets' number one. Bamford steps up himself to take the penalty, thumping a left-foot shot into the top-right corner to make it 1-0 at Elland Road.

6

25 October 1995
Leeds United v PSV Eindhoven, UEFA Cup second round, first leg

United get off to a dream start against Dutch giants PSV Eindhoven at Elland Road. When Gary McAllister is scythed down midway inside the PSV half, it gives the Scottish maestro a chance to float a free kick in from the left flank. His delivery is superb, with the pace of the ball meaning that Gary Speed needs only make the slightest connection to glance the ball into the bottom-right corner from 12 yards and put the Whites 1-0 up. In an extraordinary game, however, the Dutch side go on to win 5-3 and leave Howard Wilkinson's side facing a European exit.

6 March 2001
Real Madrid v Leeds United, Champions League second group stage

United grab an early lead away to Real Madrid to stun the Bernabéu. In what is Leeds' first attack of any note, Mark Viduka gets free down the right flank and spots Alan Smith's run down the centre. The Australian feeds an inch-perfect low ball into Smith's path and the young forward does the rest, sliding a low shot past the onrushing keeper from the edge of the box to make it 1-0.

11 December 2020
Leeds United v West Ham United, Premier League

When Patrick Bamford is brought down by West Ham keeper Łukasz Fabiański as he takes the ball past him, referee Michael Oliver is left with an easy decision to point to the penalty spot. Mateusz Klich steps up to take the penalty but his weak attempt is easily gathered by Fabiański and it seems the chance is gone. But VAR spot that Fabiański was marginally off his line when the kick was taken, so Klich is given a second chance – and he doesn't miss the re-take, putting the Whites 1-0 up at Elland Road.

7

9 April 1975
Barcelona v Leeds United, European Cup semi-final, second leg

In front of a partisan 110,000 crowd at the Camp Nou, United get the away goal they needed with just seven minutes on the clock to go 1-0 up against Johan Cruyff's Barcelona on the night and, crucially, 3-1 ahead on aggregate. A long ball forward is superbly nodded down to his right by Joe Jordan and as the Barça defender attempts to cut the danger out, he fluffs his lines and it bounces on into the path of the lethal Peter Lorimer who thunders a shot into the top-left corner to silence the home crowd in emphatic style.

24 December 1995
Leeds United v Manchester United, Premier League

In what will be a Christmas Eve classic for Leeds fans, Gary McAllister thumps the Whites ahead from the penalty spot in front of a near-40,000 Elland Road crowd. Howard Wilkinson's side came into the game on the back of a 6-2 derby drubbing away to Sheffield Wednesday, so an early spot-kick is the perfect chance to erase that nightmare result and McAllister doesn't disappoint, dispatching the ball into the top-right corner – even though Peter Schmeichel has guessed the right way – to make it 1-0.

29 December 2010
Leeds United v Portsmouth, Championship

Max Gradel bags his fifth goal in four games to put promotion-chasing United 1-0 up against Portsmouth at Elland Road. Paul Connolly's excellent ball across the six-yard box finds Gradel, who plants a right-foot shot past the keeper to put the Whites in early control.

4 July 2020
Blackburn Rovers v Leeds United, Championship

Mateusz Klich's razor-sharp awareness in the Blackburn Rovers half sets up the opening goal for United at Ewood Park. Klich catches Lewis Travers unaware as he nicks the ball away from him and then feeds a short pass into the path of Patrick Bamford, who immediately sweeps a low shot past the keeper from the edge of the box to make it 1-0 to the Championship leaders.

8

9 January 2000
Manchester City v Leeds United, FA Cup third round

In a breathless start to the clash between City and Leeds at Maine Road, United level after falling behind to a second-minute Shaun Goater header. The equaliser comes when a free kick on the left of the City box is headed downwards by Ian Harte and Eirik Bakke's minimal flick is enough to divert the ball between Ian Bishop and keeper Nicky Weaver on the line and make it 1-1.

9

26 March 1970
Manchester United v Leeds United, FA Cup semi-final second replay

After close to four hours of goalless football, Leeds finally break the deadlock against Manchester United. The teams had already ground out two gruelling FA Cup semi-finals with 0-0 draws at Hillsborough and Villa Park, before a third and ultimately decisive encounter at Bolton Wanderers' Burnden Park. The only goal of the game comes early as Allan Clarke heads down a high ball towards Mick Jones, but the danger is only half cleared by the Reds and Billy Bremner hammers a powerful shot in from 18 yards that gives Alex Stepney in goal no chance and confirms a final spot for Don Revie's talented side.

17 September 1969
Leeds United v Lyn, European Cup first round, first leg

Norwegian champions Lyn's worst fears turn into reality as a rampant Leeds go 3-0 up inside ten minutes at Elland Road. Though the first two goals had been classy efforts the visitors could do little about, the third is a scrappier affair as Billy Bremner's cross finds Mick Jones in the box and his half-volleyed shot squeezes under the keeper – who makes a hash of his attempt to keep it out – to virtually end the game as a contest with the minutes still in single figures.

29 December 2020

West Bromwich Albion v Leeds United, Premier League

A remarkable own goal gives Leeds a 1-0 lead away to West Brom. The Baggies work the ball away from their own box and it is played to Romaine Sawyers on the left – as a challenge comes in, he swivels around and plays a ball back towards his keeper without looking, but Sam Johnstone has gone to the left of the six-yard box in anticipation and the pass back is hit with too much pace and instead goes past the keeper and into the bottom-left of the goal. A bizarre own goal from fully 20 yards out.

10

30 January 1970
Manchester City v Leeds United, First Division

Title hopefuls Leeds take an early lead against Manchester City on a mud bath of a Maine Road pitch. With 43,517 fans inside the stadium to witness this War of the Roses, United strike first when Terry Cooper's howitzer of a shot is parried by Joe Corrigan and Allan Clarke lives up to his nickname of 'Sniffer' as he magically appears to prod home from close range.

5 March 1975
Leeds United v Anderlecht, European Cup quarter-final, first leg

Looking to establish a healthy advantage to take over to Belgium, United strike early against Anderlecht. With a packed Elland Road desperate for Leeds to finally reach their full potential in Europe's premier competition, a blanket of fog envelops the ground and few of the 43,000-plus crowd inside are ever aware that Joe Jordan has given the Whites the lead. Norman Hunter's excellent threaded ball sends Jordan clear on the right of the box and his angled low drive is fluffed by keeper Jan Ruiter to make it 1-0.

6 March 1996
Queens Park Rangers v Leeds United, Premier League

Tony Yeboah puts out-of-sorts Leeds 1-0 up away to QPR at Loftus Road. The Whites have travelled to London on the back of four straight Premier League losses, despite progressing well in both the FA Cup and League Cup. Andy Gray provides the assist and Yeboah finishes clinically to give Howard Wilkinson's men an early lead.

15 May 2008
Carlisle United v Leeds United, League One play-off semi-final, second leg

After a miserable first-leg defeat to Carlisle United at Elland Road, Leeds are determined to give the Cumbrian side a much sterner test on their own soil. The Whites' early enterprise is quickly rewarded when David Prutton finds Jermaine Beckford who flicks the ball on to Johnny Howson. Howson finds Dougie Freedman on the left and he returns the ball into Howson's run for the youngster to control with his chest before slotting past the keeper to make it 1-0.

27 June May 2020
Leeds United v Fulham, Championship

Leeds grab an early lead against promotion rivals Fulham at Elland Road. On a sunny June afternoon in Yorkshire, with no fans allowed in due to the ongoing pandemic restrictions, the Whites look to end the Cottagers' hopes of a top-two spot with victory and a fine burst down the right by Hélder Costa sees his low cross swept home by Patrick Bamford from 12 yards to make it 1-0.

29 December 2010
Leeds United v Portsmouth, Championship

United's blistering start threatens to blow Portsmouth away as Jonny Howson makes it 2-0 with just ten minutes played at Elland Road. Ross McCormack is the creator, finding the Leeds skipper with a pinpoint cross and Howson does the rest, firing a powerful drive past keeper Jamie Ashdown to leave the visitors reeling on the ropes.

11

7 October 1967
Leeds United v Chelsea, First Division

United double the lead over Chelsea at Elland Road. The managerless visitors are still reeling from Albert Johanneson's early strike when Peter Lorimer sets up Jimmy Greenhoff to finish from close range and make it 2-0.

9 April 1975
Leeds United v Barcelona, European Cup semi-final, first leg

An unforgettable night for Leeds on the biggest stage in club football. A superbly crafted opening goal sends more than 50,000 Leeds fans into wonderland as the Whites go 1-0 up against a Barcelona side containing the legendary Dutch stars Johan Cruyff and Johan Neeskens. It's the perfect start to the semi-final, with United needing to take some sort of advantage back to the Camp Nou. Johnny Giles spots Joe Jordan on the edge of the Catalans' box and flights a ball towards him. Jordan expertly guides a header on to Billy Bremner in space just inside the box and the diminutive Scot waits for the ball to land in his path before unleashing a rocket past the keeper and into the top-left corner to send Elland Road wild.

10 November 2002
West Ham United v Leeds United, Premier League

Leeds go 1-0 up away to West Ham with a route-one goal. Ian Pearce misjudges a huge Paul Robinson kick and as

the ball bounces, Harry Kewell is quick to follow it over
Pearce into the box, and as David James rushes off his
line, Kewell chips it over and into the middle where Nick
Barmby dives in ahead of a back-tracking defender to put
the Whites in command at Upton Park.

12

3 June 1971
Leeds United v Juventus, Inter-Cities Fairs Cup Final, second leg

United take an early lead against Italian giants Juventus to go 3-2 up on aggregate at Elland Road. It will prove a crucial goal, too, as Billy Bremner's free kick on the left of the box is aimed towards Jack Charlton and, though he doesn't win it cleanly, his challenge sees a loose ball fall to Peter Lorimer whose shot is blocked. But Allan Clarke picks it up, and hits a smart low drive into the bottom-left corner to make it 1-0 on the night. Though the Old Lady level eight minutes later, the Whites get the 1-1 draw that means the away goals in Turin secure the Inter-Cities Fairs Cup for the second time in the club's history. A fantastic night for all concerned with Leeds United Football Club and particularly the 42,000-plus crowd packed inside the ground.

5 April 2003
Charlton Athletic v Leeds United, Premier League

On the back of six successive losses and heading towards the Premier League trapdoor, United travel to in-form Charlton Athletic in what is caretaker manager Peter Reid's second game in charge. Reid makes several changes to the side that ran out at The Valley and it is quickly obvious that the new boss has identified where some of the issues lie as the Whites dominate from the word go. Mark Viduka finds Alan Smith on his left and his low cross is converted by Harry Kewell, who side-foots home from close range to make it 1-0.

12 September 2020
Liverpool v Leeds United, Premier League

Jack Harrison announces United's return to the Premier League with a delightful opening-day leveller against champions Liverpool. Having fallen behind to a Mo Salah penalty after just four minutes, the Whites roar back at Anfield as Harrison controls a long pass to the left flank and then moves past a defender almost in the same move before progressing inside and then drilling a low shot past Alisson to make it 1-1. Superb technique from the on-loan Manchester City star.

13

21 February 2001
Anderlecht v Leeds United, Champions League second group stage

Up against a side who had won their previous 21 home games in all competitions and had won nine consecutive home European matches over a longer period of time, Leeds travelled to Belgium in the Champions League second group stage expecting nothing less than a stiff examination. But on what will be a famous night for the Whites, David O'Leary's team strike first. Ian Harte's throw-in finds Alan Smith, who nods on to Mark Viduka. The Australian manages to keep the ball in play and then crosses into the box where Eirik Bakke steps over the ball and Smith is on hand to drive a low shot past keeper Zvonko Milojević from ten yards.

22 July 2020
Leeds United v Charlton Athletic, Championship

On-loan Brighton centre-back Ben White scores his only Leeds goal with a stunning strike against Charlton Athletic. With the Whites already crowned champions as the latest-ever finish to a season concludes at Elland Road, Pablo Hernández's cross from the right flank is cleared to the edge of the box where White controls it and then sends a volley into the top-right corner to make it 1-0 for United.

8 May 2021
Leeds United v Tottenham Hotspur, Premier League

United go 1-0 up against Spurs at Elland Road with more than a slice of good fortune – not that anybody inside the stadium (other than a couple of thousand travelling fans) cares a jot. As a cross from the left comes into the Spurs box, defender Sergio Reguilón doesn't know whether to stick or twist and gets a foot on the ball, forcing Hugo Lloris into a smart save down to his left, but the Frenchman can only push the ball into the path of Stuart Dallas who gleefully sweeps home from a couple of yards out to put his team ahead.

14

7 October 1967
Leeds United v Chelsea, First Division

Things go from bad to worse for Chelsea at Elland Road as a rampant United score a third goal inside the opening 14 minutes. Driven by a thirst to avenge a painful FA Cup semi-final defeat to the Londoners five months previously, the Whites sniff blood as the shell-shocked and disorganised visitors are all at sea when Eddie Gray's corner is badly misjudged by Peter Bonetti and Jack Charlton nods the ball home to make it 3-0. Suddenly, Chelsea's decision to part company with the enigmatic Tommy Docherty doesn't look such a wise decision.

12 April 1987
Coventry City v Leeds United, FA Cup semi-final

David Rennie powers United in front against the Sky Blues at a raucous and passionate Hillsborough. With the Whites looking to reach a first FA Cup final for 14 years, it is the ideal start against a Coventry side who had won their quarter-final at Hillsborough the round before, beating hosts Sheffield Wednesday 3-1. A corner from the left is powerfully headed down and past keeper Steve Ogrizovic by Rennie to make it 1-0 and send half of the ground into a frenzy in the South Yorkshire sunshine.

20 April 2000
Leeds United v Galatasaray, UEFA Cup semi-final, second leg

Though a fifth-minute goal from the Turkish side has made the task of overturning a 3-0 aggregate seem like mission impossible, United stick to the task and quickly find a way back into the tie. Jason Wilcox's curling delivery finds Eirik Bakke unmarked at the near post and his excellent glancing header flies into the top-right corner to make it 1-1 at a partisan and raucous Elland Road.

13 May 2001
Leeds United v Bradford City, Premier League

Still smarting from a midweek Champions League exit, Unite refocus and begin to take their frustration out on Yorkshire neighbours Bradford City at Elland Road. When Ian Harte is allowed too much time to cut back in on the left and cross towards the six-yard box, the Bantams are punished as Mark Viduka is first to the ball and lashes a header across the keeper and into the far corner to put the Whites 1-0 up and claim his 23rd goal of a fine season.

1 October 2011
Leeds United v Portsmouth, Championship

Danny Pugh scores what proves to be the only goal of the game to see off Portsmouth at Elland Road. Promotion-chasing United go in front when Pugh – making his second Leeds debut after arriving on loan from Stoke City – loses marker Greg Halford before planting a header home to seal a 1-0 win and send the Whites to within three points of the play-off berths with several games in hand.

15

11 April 1964
Swansea Town v Leeds United, Second Division

Needing a win to regain top-flight status, Don Revie's expertly assembled side travels to South Wales looking to secure promotion in style. The hosts hold out for quarter of an hour before Leeds break the deadlock when Terry Cooper's left-flank cross is headed home by Alan Peacock to make it 1-0 at the Vetch Field.

17 March 1973
Leeds United v Rapid Bucharest, European Cup Winners' Cup quarter-final, first leg

Johnny Giles opens the scoring at Elland Road on a night that will all but guarantee Leeds a place in the semi-finals. The elegant Irishman's goal comes after a Norman Hunter free kick into the box is punched clear by Bucharest keeper Rică Răducanu – but the ball falls to Giles who sends a sumptuous chip back over Răducanu's head and into the net to give the Whites a 1-0 first leg lead against the Romanians.

17 August 2002
Leeds United v Manchester City, Premier League

Terry Venables' Leeds get the 2002/03 campaign up and running with an early goal against Kevin Keegan's newly promoted Manchester City. With more than 40,000 inside a sun-drenched Elland Road, the Whites strike when Lee

Bowyer's clever ball into the box finds Nick Barmby who nips in ahead of City keeper Carlo Nash to prod home and make it 1-0.

19 October 2009
Leeds United v Norwich City, League One

Unbeaten United edge ahead against League One promotion rivals Norwich. Both fallen giants are desperate to escape the third tier, but it is Simon Grayson's Leeds who are making a better fist of doing so. With just 11 games played, the Whites went into the game seven points clear of the Canaries having played one fewer game, so there is plenty at stake – and when Robert Snodgrass sends in a deep corner to the back post, Bradley Johnson is there to nod home and put the Whites 1-0 up at Elland Road.

27 January 2013
Leeds United v Tottenham Hotspur, FA Cup fourth round

United grab the lead against Spurs at Elland Road. Luke Varney is sent clear on the left flank and uses his pace to head into the Spurs box unchallenged. As he angles in towards goal, he opens his body and curls a low shot past the keeper and into the bottom-right corner to give the Championship Whites a shock lead.

5 August 2018
Leeds United v Stoke City, Championship

Brilliant work by Samuel Sáiz sets up the opening goal for Leeds at Elland Road as the Whites look to get Marcelo Bielsa's tenure off to a flying start. Sáiz collects the ball on the left flank and moves inside, skipping past one challenge and then another before threading a pass to Mateusz Klich, who is onside and, after controlling the ball, he stabs it past the keeper to make it 1-0.

29 December 2019
Birmingham City v Leeds United, Championship

A fast counter-attack results in United taking the lead at St Andrew's. Jack Harrison collects a loose ball following Liam Cooper's clearance and surges forward before threading Hélder Costa through. Harrison spins off Maxime Colin before burying a low shot to the keeper's left to put the Whites 1-0 up.

31 January 2021
Leicester City v Leeds United, Premier League

United take just two minutes to level against Leicester City at the King Power Stadium after Harvey Barnes had struck for the hosts. In a lovely, flowing move down the right flank, Luke Ayling passes into the advancing Patrick Bamford's feet and he nudges it on to Stuart Dallas, who sweeps a low drive into the bottom-left corner for a superbly worked equaliser.

16

20 April 1974
Leeds United v Ipswich Town, First Division

A breathtaking goal sets Leeds off on the day that will eventually clinch a second First Division title for Don Revie's brilliant side. United had survived a hiccup on the title run-in with a poor run of form that allowed Liverpool back into the race. The visitors were looking to cement a place in the UEFA Cup and were in no mood to gift the Whites anything, but there is nothing they can do about the opening goal. Gordon McQueen wins possession just inside the Ipswich half and the ball deflects out to Peter Lorimer on the right flank. Lorimer cuts in towards the corner of the box and, with everyone expecting a cross, the Leeds winger unleashes a ferocious strike that bends away from keeper Paul Cooper and into the top-right corner of the net. A brilliant goal by the Scot with the thunderbolt shot.

17

6 April 1974
Leeds United v Derby County, First Division

Desperate to revive their flagging title hopes, Leeds know nothing but victory over Derby will do at a packed Elland Road. The Whites' hopes had taken a dip after a disappointing set of results, but the rivalry with Derby brings the best out in Don Revie's side who strike first on 17 minutes with a goal that smacks of class. The move begins when Trevor Cherry plays a short ball back to Norman Hunter, who spots Joe Jordan midway inside the Rams' half. Hunter's lofted 40-yard pass is cleverly nodded sideways by the Scotland striker to Billy Bremner, who then plays the bouncing ball into Peter Lorimer's path. Lorimer spots the keeper rushing off his line and immediately sends a lob over his head and into the net to make it 1-0.

23 May 2021
Leeds United v West Bromwich Albion, Premier League

United take the lead against relegated West Brom at Elland Road. With 8,000 fans allowed to watch as pandemic restrictions ease – the first time those Leeds supporters have seen top-flight football on home soil for 17 years – Raphinha's cross from the right to the far post is headed home by Rodrigo to make it 1-0 on the final day of a memorable return to the Premier League for Marcelo Bielsa's side.

18

15 April 1972
Leeds United v Birmingham City, FA Cup semi-final

At a packed Hillsborough, United take the lead with a typically incisive move that cuts Birmingham to shreds. It begins with Johnny Giles bringing the ball forward from the back before finding Mick Jones. Jones feeds Billy Bremner on the left and he spots Paul Reaney's run down the right. Reaney then plays Peter Lorimer in on the corner of the box for the Scot to deliver a fine cross to the back post for Allan Clarke. His cushioned header across goal is thumped home by the head of Mick Jones to make it 1-0.

19

11 April 1964

Swansea Town v Leeds United, Second Division

A second goal in the space of four minutes puts Leeds firmly in command and on the way to promotion against Swansea at the Vetch Field. Knowing victory will ensure that the Whites return to the top flight after a four-year absence, Don Revie's men go for the kill early and reap the rewards as Bobby Collins's corner is glanced home by Johnny Giles to make it 2-0.

13 May 2001

Leeds United v Bradford City, Premier League

United race into a 2-0 lead against Bradford City at Elland Road. The Bantams must fear the worst when they concede a free kick some 20 yards out and those concerns are confirmed as Ian Harte steps up to float a beautiful shot over the wall and double the Whites' lead in the Yorkshire derby.

3 January 2010

Manchester United v Leeds United, FA Cup third round

Jermaine Beckford stuns Old Trafford as Leeds cause a huge FA Cup upset. With no win at Old Trafford since 1981, the third-tier Whites are expected to be swept aside by serial trophy-winners Manchester United, but what will be the only goal of the game comes when Jonny Howson's excellent long ball catches the Reds out, with Beckford pulling clear of Wes Brown and, though his touch is heavy, Tomasz Kuszczak's attempt to close him down is in vain as the striker tucks it underneath the keeper and inside the far post to make it 1-0 – enough to secure a stunning win.

20

2 March 1968
Leeds United v Arsenal, League Cup Final

In a final described as 'one of the most unglamorous matches ever to grace Wembley Stadium's turf', United grab what will be the only goal of the game and win their first domestic trophy. A corner on the right is floated to the near post where a combination of Jack Charlton and Jimmy Greenhoff manages to impede Gunners keeper Jim Furnell and the ball drops to Terry Cooper who hammers a powerful shot home from eight yards to make it 1-0 to Don Revie's side. The Whites opt to grind out the victory rather than looking for more goals, but half of the 97,887 crowd couldn't give two hoots because the trophy hoodoo is finally over.

17 September 1969
Leeds United v Lyn, European Cup first round, first leg

United go 4-0 up against Lyn with a classy goal from record signing Allan Clarke. Collecting a high ball out of defence, Clarke effortlessly drifts past three defenders into the box before drilling a low shot beyond the keeper from eight yards to further punish the Norwegian amateurs at Elland Road.

20 April 1970
Chelsea v Leeds United, FA Cup Final

Chasing that elusive first FA Cup triumph, United strike first in the 1970 final. On a pitch resembling a cabbage patch, the opening goal comes from a set piece as Eddie Gray swings a corner from the right into the six-yard box where Jack Charlton muscles his way in to head the ball down. The two Chelsea players on the line are powerless to clear as it drops between them and rolls about a foot over the line to make it 1-0 to Don Revie's side in front of a 100,000 Wembley crowd.

9 January 2000
Manchester City v Leeds United, FA Cup third round

In a rip-roaring cup tie at Maine Road, United level for the second time inside the first 20 minutes. Again, City have conceded a needless free kick, this time on the right – and from the resulting cross, United equalise as Ian Harte heads the ball goalwards and, despite a fine reflex save by keeper Nicky Weaver, Alan Smith bundles home from point-blank range to make it 2-2.

8 December 2009
Leeds United v Kettering Town, FA Cup second round replay

Luciano Becchio heads Leeds in front against non-League Kettering at a sparsely populated Elland Road. With the game live on TV, the fans largely stay away from a game United are expected to win easily, and when Becchio makes it 1-0 it seems that's how things will pan out. Becchio feeds Robert Snodgrass on the left of the box and he cuts back inside and lofts a cross into the middle for the Argentine to nod into the bottom-right corner. However, the visitors dig in and level just past the hour-mark to eventually force extra time.

29 November 2011
Nottingham Forest v Leeds United, Championship

Just two days after the news that Gary Speed had died, an emotional Leeds took to the field at Nottingham Forest's City Ground. With Simon Grayson's side determined to give the former Whites legend a fitting send-off, Robert Snodgrass cracks a long-range effort into the bottom-right corner and past Lee Camp in the Forest goal to make it 1-0 and set up a memorable evening for all United fans.

21

11 August 2018
Derby County v Leeds United, Championship

Having seen an early lead cancelled out, United go back in front against Frank Lampard's Derby at Pride Park. It's a superb goal, too, as Ezgjan Alioski skips down the left flank before delivering a quality cross that Kemar Roofe leaps to head into the corner from eight yards and make it 2-1.

29 December 2019
Birmingham City v Leeds United, Championship

Leeds' superb start at St Andrew's continues as Jack Harrison doubles their advantage. Harrison cracks a half-volley towards goal after being teed up by Ezgjan Alioski and sees his effort take a sizeable deflection off Harlee Dean to wrong-foot Connal Trueman in goal and put Marcelo Bielsa's men 2-0 up.

22

20 April 1974
Leeds United v Ipswich Town, First Division

United go 2-0 up in the potential title-clincher against Ipswich Town at Elland Road. The Whites win a free kick when Brian Talbot handles on the edge of the box as he attempts to make a clearance. Peter Lorimer, scorer of a stunning opener just six minutes earlier, thumps the set piece towards goal and Paul Cooper dives to his right to make a fine save, but as the ball loops up, Billy Bremner is first to react, sending a diving header into the net to double the champions-elect's lead. Ipswich defenders protest long and loud – with justification – that Bremner had been in an offside position when Lorimer struck the ball, but with VAR still decades away, the goal stands.

23

9 May 1973
Leeds United v Arsenal, First Division

After suffering the ignominy of defeat to Second Division Sunderland in the FA Cup Final a few days before, United are determined to end the league campaign on a high. Facing runners-up Arsenal at Elland Road, Don Revie's side were already guarantee third spot in the table, but with a European Cup Winners' Cup Final to come against AC Milan, it was imperative that they rediscovered their form against the Gunners. And for all the disappointments of what could have been a treble-winning campaign, the Whites turn on the style. The opening goal comes when Joe Jordan is wrestled to the ground in the box by Brendan Batson, giving the referee an easy decision in pointing to the spot. The Arsenal players react angrily and insist the official consult his linesman – which he does – but there is no change of heart and Peter Lorimer places the ball on the spot before thumping it past Bob Wilson to make it 1-0.

24

15 April 1972
Leeds United v Birmingham City, FA Cup semi-final

Leeds' superb start is rewarded with a second goal with less than 25 minutes played at Hillsborough. Mick Jones, scorer of the opening goal, finds Eddie Gray on the left flank and he plays a superb long ball into the path of Peter Lorimer. After holding off a challenge from the defender, Lorimer sends a low, angled shot past the keeper and just inside the left-hand post to put the Whites 2-0 up against Birmingham City.

15 May 2019
Leeds United v Derby County, Championship play-off semi-final, second leg

Stuart Dallas taps the ball home to put United 1-0 up against Derby and, crucially, 2-0 up on aggregate. At a packed Elland Road, the opener comes when a cross from the left is headed against the inside of the post by Liam Cooper, but the ball bounces kindly to Dallas who can't miss from a couple of yards out.

25

6 March, 1996
Queens Park Rangers v Leeds United, Premier League

If there was one bright spark in a largely disappointing season for United, it was Tony Yeboah. Adored by the Leeds faithful, the Ghanaian scores what will be his last league goal for the Whites to open up a 2-0 lead at QPR. It's his 12th league goal of the campaign and, though the Hoops will pull one back five minutes later, it will be enough to earn three points for his side.

4 November 2000
Leeds United v Liverpool, Premier League

Trailing 2-0 to a rampant Liverpool at Elland Road, Leeds find a way back into the game thanks to the persistence of the tenacious Alan Smith. Christian Ziege looks to have plenty of time to clear the ball upfield, but Smith closes him down and the German sees his attempted pass deflected to Mark Viduka in the Liverpool box. The Australian clips a delightful chip over the keeper to halve the deficit.

26

8 August 1992
Leeds United v Liverpool, FA Charity Shield

Leeds open the scoring at Wembley with a counter-attack goal against Liverpool. Rod Wallace bursts clear down the left before checking his run in the Reds' box. He looks to his right and tees up Eric Cantona, who plants a rising right-foot shot past Bruce Grobbelaar to make it 1-0.

4 April 2000
Leeds United v Deportivo La Coruña, Champions League quarter-final, first leg

Leeds go ahead as dreams of European glory continue at Elland Road. The opener comes from a set piece as Ian Harte strikes a curling left-foot free kick over the Deportivo wall, beyond the keeper and into the roof of the net to send the United fans wild.

13 May 2001
Leeds United v Bradford City, Premier League

A splendid move cuts Bradford apart as United go 3-1 up at Elland Road. The Bantams had just pulled a goal back against the run of play, put David O'Leary's men resume control as Alan Smith plays a superb threaded pass to Eirik Bakke, who runs on before dispatching a powerful, angled drive into the roof of the net with the outside of his right boot.

27

9 May 1973
Leeds United v Arsenal, First Division

United quickly double their lead against Arsenal at Elland Road with Peter Lorimer's second of the afternoon. Allan Clarke's fine work sees him find Billy Bremner, who holds the ball up before laying it off to the overlapping Lorimer and the Scottish winger makes no mistake with a superb finish into the top-left corner to make it 2-0.

2 May 2004
Bolton Wanderers v Leeds United, Premier League

Needing a win to have any realistic chance of avoiding relegation, United take the lead against Bolton at the Reebok Stadium. Emerson Thome misjudges a long Paul Robinson goal kick and bundles over Alan Smith, giving the referee no choice but to award a penalty. Mark Viduka slots home to make it 1-0 and give the many thousands of United fans a glimmer of hope.

28

17 March 1973
Leeds United v Rapid Bucharest, European Cup Winners' Cup quarter-final, first leg

Allan Clarke doubles United's lead against Rapid at Elland Road – and it is a superbly choreographed move that undoes the Romanians. Norman Hunter finds Johnny Giles, who looks up and flights the ball to Joe Jordan. His guided header is into the path of Clarke, who gives the keeper no chance with a typically classy finish.

10 November 2002
West Ham United v Leeds United, Premier League

Leeds go back in front against West Ham at Upton Park. It's a fairly straightforward set-piece goal, with Ian Harte's out-swinging cross from the left met on the corner of the six-yard box by Harry Kewell, who sends a smart header back across keeper David James to put the Whites 2-1 up.

16 July 2020
Leeds United v Barnsley, Championship

The relatively unknown Michael Sollbauer is responsible for the goal that takes United to within one point of a Premier League return. The Whites, hosting bottom side Barnsley, get what will be the only goal of the South Yorkshire derby as Tykes defender Sollbauer turns Patrick Bamford's pull-back past his own keeper to make it 1-0 at Elland Road. Results elsewhere the following weekend mean this victory will prove to be enough to ensure a return to the Premier League for the first time in 16 years for Marcelo Bielsa's side.

14 March 2001
Leeds United v Lazio, Champions League second group stage
Already qualified for the quarter-finals of the Champions League at the first attempt, a weakened Leeds level against Lazio at Elland Road with a well-worked goal. Harry Kewell nods the ball inside to Lee Bowyer, who sends a fine right-foot chip over goalkeeper Luca Marchegiani to make it 1-1.

22 July 2020
Leeds United v Charlton Athletic, Championship
The champions double their lead against League One-bound Charlton Athletic. Spanish magician Pablo Hernández makes the goal as he receives the ball on the right of the Addicks' box from Stuart Dallas, who then continues his run. Hernández then sends a pass through a defender's legs and into the path of Dallas, who toe-pokes the ball past the keeper from six yards to make it 2-0 for Marcelo Bielsa's side. Brilliant from Hernández!

29

30 January 1970
Manchester City v Leeds United, First Division

Leeds take a commanding and decisive 2-0 lead against Manchester City at Maine Road. United win a corner and City only half clear the danger as far as Jack Charlton, who thumps the ball past Joe Corrigan to double the Whites' lead and give the hosts a mountain to climb – one that they won't ascend.

5 April 2010
Yeovil Town v Leeds United, League One

Having won just three of the past 15 matches – seven of which ended in defeat – United's massive promotion wobble looks set to end miserably. Victory away to Yeovil was crucial. Simon Grayson's side had gone from runaway leaders, whose 2-1 win over Norwich City earlier in the campaign had seen them go 11 points clear of the Canaries, to trailing champions-elect Norwich by 11 points with just six games to go. It was a familiar tale of woe for the long-suffering Whites fans, who fully expected their side to dip out of the top six all together – but skipper Richard Naylor has other ideas as his looping header from Jonny Howson's cross drops over the keeper and into the net to make it 1-0 for the visitors at Huish Park. It is United's first goal in more than six hours of football.

30

12 September 2020
Liverpool v Leeds United, Premier League

Patrick Bamford equalises for Leeds, who peg back champions Liverpool at Anfield for the second time on the opening day of the 2020/21 campaign. The Whites, exchanging punches with the Reds on their home turf, make it 2-2 when Virgil van Dijk attempts to control a cross into the box but a poor first touch sees the Dutch defender present the ball to Bamford, who accepts the gift by tucking past Alisson from eight yards.

31

14 November 2002
Hapoel Tel Aviv v Leeds United, UEFA Cup second round, second leg

Having conceded a second-minute goal in the second leg of the UEFA Cup second round, and also having seen a 1-0 first-leg lead erased, Alan Smith begins his one-man dismantling of the Hapoel Tel Aviv defence as he levels the scores in Israel as well as bagging a vital away goal. Erik Bakke's flick gives Smith just enough room to squeeze a shot past the keeper from a tight angle to change the complexion of the tie completely.

29 December 2020
West Bromwich Albion v Leeds United, Premier League

United double their lead away to West Brom with a stunning strike. If the opening goal had been fortuitous, the second is a beauty as a cross into the Baggies' box is cleared to the left where it falls to Ezgjan Alioski, who thumps a howitzer of a left-foot drive into the top-right corner from 18 yards out to make it 2-0 to the Whites.

32

5 May 1973
Leeds United v Sunderland, FA Cup final

One of the darkest days in Leeds United's history as Second Division Sunderland score what will be the only goal of the final. With Don Revie's side red-hot favourites to win the competition for only the second time in the club's history – and this after having finally won it the season before – Bob Stokoe's spirited Mackems grab the lead as a corner is chested down by Vic Hallom and the ball falls into the path of Ian Porterfield, who takes a touch before hammering a shot into the roof of the net from six yards out. United's Achilles heel of failing to see the most important games through strikes again as Sunderland win 1-0.

23 September 1995
Wimbledon v Leeds United, Premier League

Carlton Palmer scores a superb 20-yard shot into the top-right corner to put Leeds 1-0 up away to Wimbledon. The gangly midfielder takes the ball towards the Dons' box before checking back inside a challenge and then firing a wonderful curling drive that Paul Heald has no chance of stopping.

33

31 March 2001
Sunderland v Leeds United, Premier League
United go ahead at the Stadium of Light with a well-worked opener. Ian Harte clips in a cross from the left that finds Harry Kewell unmarked and in space at the back post. Kewell guides a header back to the edge of the six-yard box where Alan Smith is waiting to nod past Thomas Sørensen and open up a 1-0 lead.

2 May 2004
Bolton Wanderers v Leeds United, Premier League
Having given Leeds fans slender hope of avoiding the drop, Mark Viduka is then responsible for ending that optimism. Just six minutes after stroking home a penalty, and with tempers fraying, the Australian is first booked for kicking Emerson Thome, and then flings an arm in Bruno N'Gotty's face after which he is shown a second yellow and dismissed. It will be his last act for Leeds, who go on to lose 4-1 and are relegated from the top flight.

8 May 2010
Leeds United v Bristol Rovers, League One
An explosive few minutes begin after a Jermaine Beckford goal is disallowed and, from a resulting melee, Max Gradel is shown a straight red card in a game United need to win to secure promotion from League One. It is unclear what exactly happens, but the referee sends Gradel off and the

player has to be restrained by his team-mates as he reacts furiously to the official. With the score at 0-0 and Elland Road at fever pitch, it is the last thing manager Simon Grayson wants and it is several minutes before Gradel walks off with the Whites needing a monumental effort now to get the three points needed

34

11 April 1964
Swansea Town v Leeds United, Second Division

United's task of victory in South Wales to secure promotion back to the top flight looks complete with barely half an hour played against Swansea as goal number three goes in at the Vetch Field. Terry Cooper's corner finds Johnny Giles, who fires a shot home via Swans defender Roy Evans to make it 3-0 and secure the two points Don Revie's emerging side need.

17 September 1969
Leeds United v Lyn, European Cup first round, first leg

Leeds' ruthless dismantling of Lyn ensures that nobody will forget the Whites' first European Cup tie. Having managed to go 14 minutes without conceding, the visitors can do nothing about United's fifth of the first half as Johnny Giles moves forward with purpose before deciding to have a crack from distance – and what a shot it is, a howitzer of a drive from 20 yards that flies into the top-left corner to make it 5-0.

27 September 1997
Leeds United v Manchester United, Premier League

David Wetherall scores what will be the only goal of an explosive encounter between Leeds and Manchester United. The Whites had created more and been in the faces of the Reds at a packed Elland Road, but it isn't until the 34th minute that George Graham's side finally break through as Gary Kelly's set piece from the right floats into the six-yard box and Wetherall gets above Gary Pallister to head firmly past Peter Schmeichel and make it 1-0. Cue scenes of pandemonium around the stadium.

21 February 2001
Anderlecht v Leeds United, Champions League second group stage

Leeds extend their lead away to Anderlecht. The move that brings the Whites' second goal starts with Olivier Dacourt feeding Dominic Matteo on the left, and he sends a deep cross towards the back post where Mark Viduka gets up to loop a header up and over the keeper to make it 2-0 as the Australian striker ends a run of nine games without a goal.

5 April 2003
Charlton Athletic v Leeds United, Premier League

United go 2-0 up away to Charlton Athletic as temporary boss Peter Reid oversees an excellent display at The Valley. The second goal comes from the penalty spot as Richard Rufus hauls down Alan Smith in the box and Ian Harte steps up to double the Whites' lead against Alan Curbishley's Europe-chasing outfit.

5 April 2010
Yeovil Town v Leeds United, League One

Richard Naylor makes his own case for being Captain Fantastic as he heads his struggling side into a vital 2-0 lead at Huish Park. The skipper had opened the scoring just five minutes earlier and he repeats the feat as he nods home Neil Kilkenny's corner for his second of the game. Though the hosts will halve the deficit in the second half and press hard for a leveller, Leeds hang on to win 2-1 and end a run of four successive defeats.

35

20 April 1970
Chelsea v Leeds United, FA Cup Final replay

In yet another tinderbox atmosphere between Chelsea and Leeds, it is United who take the lead for the third time over the course of the final and the replay at Manchester United's Old Trafford. And once again it is Mick Jones who scores, picking the ball up midway inside the Chelsea half before driving towards the edge of the box where he fires a rising, angled shot past Peter Bonetti and into the left-hand corner of the net to make it 1-0.

17 March 1973
Leeds United v Rapid Bucharest, European Cup Winners' Cup quarter-final, first leg

The Whites continue to run riot against Rapid Bucharest at Elland Road with a third first-half goal. Yet again, the intelligence and technique of Don Revie's side is too much for the Romanians to cope with as Allan Clarke cleverly diverts a header into space for Peter Lorimer to unleash a thunderous drive from ten yards out to give keeper Rică Răducanu no chance and make the score 3-0. So powerful is the Scotland winger's shot that, had the keeper got in the way, he'd have likely ended up in the back of the net with the ball!

16 December 2020

Leeds United v Newcastle United, Premier League

Leeds level at Elland Road against Newcastle with a Patrick Bamford header. When a cross comes into the Magpies' box from the right, Raphinha manages to direct a header on target as it loops up and over the keeper – but as it bounces off the top of the bar, Bamford is on hand to nod home from a yard out, making the score 1-1.

36

1 October 2016
Leeds United v Barnsley, Championship

Barnsley defender Sam Winnall is at odds with his surname as he allows Kyle Bartley to spin off him and head home Pablo Hernandez's corner to put the Whites 1-0 up at Elland Road in this Yorkshire derby clash. United will go on to win the game 2-1, giving Garry Monk's side a fourth league win in five as a dreadful start to the campaign is steadily erased.

37

28 April 1962
Newcastle United v Leeds United, Second Division

New Leeds boss Don Revie was gradually guiding the Whites to safety but despite an unbeaten run of eight games – two wins and six draws – a point was still needed on the final day of the season with a difficult trip to Newcastle to negotiate. The Revie era had begun and, against a Magpies side with little to play for, Billy McAdams crosses for Albert Johanneson to thump a shot in off the underside of the crossbar and give Leeds a vital 1-0 lead.

3 March 1972
Leeds United v Southampton, First Division

Leeds finally grab a well-deserved goal to go ahead against Southampton. Billy Bremner finds Eddie Gray on the halfway line and plays it into his path. Gray plays a neat one-two with Mick Jones on the edge of the box and then plays it left to Allan Clarke, who hits a low shot that beats the keeper and is helped into the net by the despairing lunge of a defender to make it 1-0.

24 December 1995
Leeds United v Manchester United, Premier League

Leeds go back in front against Manchester United with a terrific Tony Yeboah goal. Latching on to a Tomas Brolin pass, Yeboah has four defenders around him but he shimmies himself some space, tormenting Denis Irwin before hitting a low drive into the bottom-left corner from just inside the Reds' box to make it 2-1 at Elland Road.

13 May 2001
Leeds United v Bradford City, Premier League

It's a Yorkshire derby to forget for Bradford as Leeds cruise into a 4-1 first-half lead at Elland Road. The Whites, chasing a top-four finish and Champions League football again, are just too hot for the Bantams as Danny Mills's lofted cross to the back post finds Mark Viduka, who gently nods down to Alan Smith to volley a low shot home from six yards an end the game as a contest.

38

7 October 1967
Leeds United v Chelsea, First Division

A purring Leeds go 4-0 up against Chelsea at Elland Road. Having swept into a 3-0 lead inside the opening 14 minutes, United are made to wait a bit longer to increase the advantage and seal victory with seven minutes of the first half still to play. The fourth is the result of a superb team move that ends with Peter Lorimer sending a thunderous drive from an angle that gives Peter Bonetti no chance.

21 February 2001
Anderlecht v Leeds United, Champions League second group stage

United are in dreamland with a third goal away to Anderlecht. The manager of the Belgian side had inadvertently fired up the Whites after the first meeting at Elland Road where he had claimed he expected his team to win the return clash as Leeds were 'not a strong team'. But he probably reassesses that belief as his team go 3-0 down thanks to a slick passing move that ends with David Batty playing the ball to Alan Smith who sends a deft chip over the onrushing home keeper to score his second of the evening.

25 August 2009
Leeds United v Watford, League Cup second round

League One United go in front against Championship side Watford at Elland Road. Robert Snodgrass buries Mike Grella's pass into the bottom-left corner of the net to put Simon Grayson's team 1-0 up.

7 May 2011
Queens Park Rangers v Leeds United, Championship

Despite conceding after just 26 seconds, United fight back to draw level with Championship winners QPR with a goal seven minutes before the break. Richard Naylor's long ball into the Rangers box is met by Max Gradel, who nods past the keeper to silence most of a celebratory Loftus Road and make it 1-1.

29 December 2020
West Bromwich Albion v Leeds United, Premier League

Jack Harrison makes it two goals in eight minutes as United go 3-0 up at struggling West Brom. It is a superb team goal, too, as Ezgjan Alioski plays a pass to Jack Harrison who cuts in from the left before playing a neat one-two with Patrick Bamford, turning a defender and then planting a left-foot shot into the top-left corner from ten yards with a wonderful finish.

39

28 October 1995
Leeds United v Coventry City, Premier League

Gary McAllister levels for Leeds against Coventry. Dion Dublin had given the visitors a 12th-minute lead, but the Whites equalise when McAllister strikes a shot from 25 yards that takes a wicked deflection off a Coventry player, leaving the keeper flat-footed on its way into the bottom-right corner to make it 1-1.

40

4 July 2020
Blackburn Rovers v Leeds United, Championship

The Whites go 2-0 up away to Blackburn Rovers at Ewood Park. When Tyler Roberts is fouled 25 yards out, Kalvin Phillips weighs up a shot with Jack Harrison alongside him. Phillips takes the free kick, curling a beauty into the top-right corner to double the Championship leaders' advantage.

29 December 2020
West Bromwich Albion v Leeds United, Premier League

The Whites make it three goals in less than ten minutes to wrap up victory away to West Brom with five minutes of the first half still to play. The hosts' capitulation continues. It's yet another fine team goal that starts well inside the Leeds half before the ball eventually finds its way to Rodrigo on the edge of the box and his low shot strikes Dara O'Shea and wrong-foots keeper Sam Johnstone to make it 4-0 at The Hawthorns.

41

7 August 1968
Leeds United v Ferencváros, Inter-Cities Fairs Cup Final, first leg

Mick Jones scores what will be the only goal of the game against Hungarian side Ferencváros at Elland Road. With a crowd of just over 25,000 due to live BBC coverage, United go ahead when a Peter Lorimer corner sees Jack Charlton challenge keeper István Géczi and, as the ball drops down, Jones manages to force it over the line from close range. It will give the Whites a 1-0 lead to take to Hungary, which will be successfully defended in a 0-0 draw to give Don Revie's side a first major trophy following a single-goal aggregate victory.

21 August 2021
Leeds United v Everton, Premier League

With a full Elland Road witnessing a first top-flight game at Elland Road for more than 16 years, Mateusz Klich levels against Everton. Patrick Bamford wins possession inside the Everton half and then slips a short pass to his left, which Klich controls before stroking a shot into the bottom-left corner to make it 1-1, with the Leeds fans going crazy.

9 January 2000
Manchester City v Leeds United, FA Cup third round

Leeds go in front for the first time in a breathless FA Cup tie away to Manchester City. The hosts had twice seen a lead cancelled out by the Whites, but Harry Kewell's goal just before the break sends David O'Leary's men in 3-2 up at the break. A patient move sees a pass played out to Jason Wilcox and the winger's low cross is turned in at the far post by Kewell from a yard out.

10 November 2002
West Ham United v Leeds United, Premier League

Harry Kewell – already with one assist and a goal – scores his second of the first half as United go 3-1 up away to West Ham. When a right-wing cross is nodded towards Kewell on the right of the Hammers' box, he immediately hits a sweet volley into the bottom-right corner to give David James no chance.

17 January 2006
Leeds United v Wigan Athletic, FA Cup third round replay

After earning a creditable draw at the JJB Stadium, Leeds hosted Wigan looking to knock the Premier League side out of the competition. The Latics look set to go into the break leading 1-0 until United crank up the pressure with successive corners, and from the third the equaliser comes as Rob Hulse nods Gary Kelly's cross towards goal and, although Leighton Baines manages to prevent it going in the net, David Healy is on hand to poke the loose ball home.

19 September 2020
Leeds United v Fulham, Premier League

The Whites go back in front against Fulham at Elland Road after referee Anthony Taylor points to the spot for a foul on Patrick Bamford. The United striker is barged off the ball as he goes for a header and Mateusz Klich is calmness personified as he gently rolls the ball past the keeper to make it 2-1.

42

3 March 1972
Leeds United v Southampton, First Division

Leeds shift up a gear with a second goal in the space of five minutes against Southampton. Again, the Whites slice open the visitors' defence as Eddie Gray claims his second assist with a pass that sets Peter Lorimer clear and, after getting the ball under control, the Scot hits an angled low drive across the keeper and into the bottom-left corner to make it 2-0.

5 March 1975
Leeds United v Anderlecht, European Cup quarter-final, first leg

At a fog-bound Elland Road, the teams return to playing after an 18-minute period where visibility was so poor that the referee took the players off. With United already 1-0 up, the threat of abandonment is the last thing Jimmy Armfield's men need, but the fog lifts enough to re-start the game and three minutes before the break it's 2-0. A Johnny Giles free kick on the right of the box finds the head of Joe Jordan, who nods it back across the six-yard box for fellow Scot Gordon McQueen to score from close range.

23 September 1995
Wimbledon v Leeds United, Premier League

Tony Yeboah doubles United's lead away to Wimbledon, though it is the driving run from Carlton Palmer that makes the goal possible. Palmer collects a short pass from Gary McAllister before moving to the edge of the Dons' box and feeding it to his right, and the low cross that comes over is turned in at close quarters by Yeboah.

13 May 2001
Leeds United v Bradford City, Premier League
A brilliant counter-attack sees Leeds go 5-1 up before half-time as Bradford's capitulation shows no sign of ending. As so often, the Whites make the most of Paul Robinson's quick distribution and ability to kick huge balls down the pitch as he clears into Bantams territory for Harry Kewell to collect. The Australian juggles the ball as he torments his marker before drifting inside and casually rolling past the onrushing keeper.

5 April 2003
Charlton Athletic v Leeds United, Premier League
An irked Mark Viduka puts relegation-threatened Leeds 3-0 up at seventh-placed Charlton Athletic. Viduka had bickered with Ian Harte over who should take the 34th-minute penalty that Harte dispatched confidently, but Viduka puts his frustration to good use as he collects Alan Smith's nod-on and chests the ball down before firing a fierce shot across the keeper from 12 yards.

20 December 2020
Manchester United v Leeds United, Premier League
After a disastrous first 40 minutes or so, Leeds show their battling instincts as Liam Cooper heads home from a Raphina corner, with the Whites looking to at least restore

some pride. The Reds had swept into a 4-0 lead thanks to some poor defending by Marcelo Bielsa's men, but Leeds continued to play their part in an end-to-end game at Old Trafford. Cooper's header just before the break at least gives them something to try and build on.

10 April 2021
Manchester City v Leeds United, Premier League

United take a shock league against runaway Premier League leaders Manchester City with a goal just before the break. Hélder Costa attacks down the left flank before finding Patrick Bamford on the edge of the City box. Bamford plays a short pass to Stuart Dallas and his low drive strikes the foot of the left-hand post then spins into the opposite side of the net to stun a deserted Etihad Stadium.

8 May 2021
Leeds United v Tottenham Hotspur, Premier League

Leeds go back in front just before the break with Patrick Bamford making it 2-1 against Spurs at Elland Road. It's a well-worked goal, too, with Jack Harrison's clever back-heel freeing Ezgjan Alioski on the left and his low cross is poked home by Bamford from close range after a clever run to the near post leaves him space and time to finish.

43

8 August 1992
Leeds United v Liverpool, FA Charity Shield

There is more than a slice of good fortune about the goal that restores United's lead in the FA Charity Shield. A free kick is awarded slightly to the right of the Liverpool box and, though three stand over the ball, Tony Dorigo strikes a shot that hits Ronny Rosenthal's backside and arrows into the bottom-left corner to make it 2-1.

28 October 1995
Leeds United v Coventry City, Premier League

Gary McAllister scores his second goal in five minutes as Leeds go from 1-0 down to 2-1 up at Elland Road. The cultured midfielder gently lifts a free kick from the edge of the box up and over the wall and into the top-left corner with typical grace to give Howard Wilkinson's men an unexpected advantage at the break.

14 March 2001
Leeds United v Lazio, Champions League second group stage

Leeds level against Lazio in what is effectively a dead rubber – though you would never have guessed it in an increasingly bad-tempered clash. The Italians looked to be set to go in 2-1 up at the break until Gary Kelly's corner finds its way to the back post where Jason Wilcox is on hand to fire a fierce volley home.

25 October 2016
Leeds United v Norwich City, League Cup fourth round

Looking for a first appearance in the League Cup quarter-finals for 20 years, United level against Norwich. A cross from the left finds Souleymane Doukara at the far post and, when his shot is kept out by a combination of goalkeeper and defender on the line, the ball falls to Marcus Antonsson who has the simplest of tap-ins into the empty net to make it 1-1.

13 August 2019
Salford City v Leeds United, League Cup first round

On Leeds' first visit to Salford City's Peninsula Stadium, Eddie Nketiah breaks the League Two side's resistance with a simple finish just before the break. The on-loan Arsenal striker has the easiest of finishes as he taps home Hélder Costa's low cross from the right from a yard or so out to put the Whites 1-0 up.

23 May 2021
Leeds United v West Bromwich Albion, Premier League

The Whites double their lead against relegated West Brom at Elland Road. When Kalvin Phillips shapes up to take a free kick on the left, at almost 30 yards from goal it looks ambitious, but his dipping shot bounces just before the keeper and up and over into the net to make it 2-0.

44

18 March 1972
Leeds United v Tottenham Hotspur, FA Cup quarter-final

In a cracking FA Cup tie at Elland Road, Leeds level against Spurs having fallen behind just four minutes earlier. The Whites respond to the setback by peppering the visitors' goal and getting their reward on half-time. Peter Lorimer's cross finds Eddie Gray, who immediately tees up Billy Bremner, but his shot is saved by Pat Jennings. Terry Cooper's follow-up effort sees the ball eventually fall to Allan Clarke a couple of yards out and he manages to bundle it over the line for 1-1.

45

26 April 1992
Sheffield United v Leeds United, First Division

A comedy of errors leads to Leeds equalising at Bramall Lane on a day where victory could virtually confirm the Whites as top-flight champions. Rod Wallace chases a ball into the Blades' box before seeing his shot beaten away by the keeper. Two defenders fail to clear and, as one manages to hoof the ball against Gary Speed, it flies back across goal where Wallace instinctively sticks out a knee and it goes into the net despite a comical leap from another home defender to keep the ball out.

23 September 1995
Wimbledon v Leeds United, Premier League

A quite stunning strike from Tony Yeboah proves to be one that will ultimately win *Match of the Day*'s Goal of the Season award. When a high ball towards the Wimbledon box is partially cleared, it falls to Yeboah who chests it down on to his thigh, moves forward a yard then cuts inside and past two defenders before unleashing an explosive shot that crashes on to the underside of the crossbar and down then up into the roof of the net to make it 3-1. It's a wonderful goal and one of the best in the Whites' history.

17 August 2002
Leeds United v Manchester City, Premier League

United double their lead against a Manchester City side who had cruised to the second-tier title just a few months previously. Kevin Keegan's team are caught out when Nick Barmby slides Mark Viduka clear with the Blues hoping for an offside flag that never comes – Viduka doesn't wait to find out and coolly slots home past Carlo Nash to make it 2-0 for Terry Venables' men.

10 November 2002
West Ham United v Leeds United, Premier League

Things go from bad worse for West Ham as they go 4-1 down to a rampant Leeds at Upton Park. Christian Dailly's lazy, under-hit back-pass from 40 yards out leaves David James with no option but to race out and try and clear the ball, but Mark Viduka is too quick, nipping in to take it around the keeper before rolling his shot into the empty net to all but seal three points with the second period still to play. The hosts improve after the break, but Leeds still win 4-3 in east London.

29 January 2011
Nottingham Forest v Leeds United, Championship

United double their lead against Nottingham Forest with another spectacular effort. Luciano Becchio manages to flick on the ball with his head and Robert Snodgrass deftly finds Jonny Howson, who doesn't hesitate as he cracks a superb half-volley past Lee Camp from the edge of the box.

9 July 2020
Leeds United v Stoke City, Championship

Hélder Costa celebrates his permanent deal to become a Leeds player by winning a penalty on the stroke of half-time against Stoke. Costa's mazy run sees him chopped down by Tommy Smith just inside the left-hand corner of the box. Mateusz Klich strokes the spot-kick home to give the Championship leaders a 1-0 lead at the break.

45+1

29 April 2017
Leeds United v Norwich City, Championship

At a shell-shocked Elland Road, Leeds fans are filtering out for their half-time refreshments with their hopes of reaching the Championship play-offs seemingly in tatters. Norwich had raced into a 3-0 lead on a day only a victory would keep their flickering hopes of a top-six finish alive, but those still in their seats are given a flicker of hope when Stuart Dallas's low cross from the left is volleyed home by Chris Wood at the near post to make it 3-1 in first-half added time.

5 August 2018
Leeds United v Stoke City, Championship

United go 2-0 up against Stoke in first-half added time thanks to a howler from goalkeeper Jack Butland. Ezgjan Alioski collects the ball on the left before playing a short pass to Pablo Hernández, who sends a low shot in from 20 yards that seems to be easily covered by Butland as he goes down to his right. But although the England international gets two hands to the ball, it still squirms through and over the line to double the Whites' advantage.

10 April 2021
Manchester City v Leeds United, Premier League

With his side having just gone 1-0 up, United skipper Liam Cooper makes a rash challenge that leaves his team-mates with a long second half to face with just ten men. As Gabriel Jesus goes for the ball on the left wing, Cooper's over-zealous tackle is both high and dangerous and, though referee Andre Marriner initially only shows a yellow card, VAR suggests it is worth another look on the pitchside monitors, which eventually results in a straight red.

Second half

46

17 March 2001
Charlton Athletic v Leeds United, Premier League

In an extraordinary coincidence, Leeds score within a minute of the half starting for the second time against Charlton at The Valley. The Whites had gone ahead after just 11 seconds in the first half and 44 seconds into the second period, as Alan Smith puts them back in front. Harry Kewell is the creator, running half the length of the field before supplying Smith with a perfectly weighted pass and he cracks a fierce drive home from the edge of the box to make it 2-1 to Leeds with what will prove to be the winning goal.

9 February 2010
Carlisle United v Leeds United, Football League Trophy area final, second leg

Trailing 2-1 from the first leg, Leeds have gone into the break 1-0 down and 3-1 down overall. But Simon Grayson's half-time talk seems to do the trick as the Whites level against Carlisle within 40 seconds of the restart through Robert Snodgrass, giving the large travelling support of United fans renewed optimism.

47

17 September 1969
Leeds United v Lyn, European Cup first round, first leg

United bag a sixth against the Norwegian champions, who can do little to prevent the drubbing they are receiving. A free kick on the right is taken short by Paul Reaney to Billy Bremner, who sends a cross into the six-yard box for Allan Clarke to head home his second of the evening.

19 February 1972
Leeds United v Manchester United, First Division

Despite dominating the first 45, Leeds fail to break down an out-of-form Manchester United at Elland Road. There was a feeling that if the Whites could get one, the floodgates would open – and that's exactly what happens. Johnny Giles, on the left of the box, plays the ball to Allan Clarke, who makes to cross, and as he unbalances two defenders, he cuts inside and feeds a pass to Eddie Gray, whose shot is tipped on to the post by keeper Alex Stepney and Mick Jones rushes in to make sure it crosses the line.

4 November 2000
Leeds United v Liverpool, Premier League

United come from two goals down to level at 2-2 with Liverpool in a thrilling encounter at Elland Road. Gary Kelly is the creator, bustling past Patrik Berger on the right flank before curling an inviting cross into the box, where Mark Viduka is on hand to power a header home at the near post for his second goal on what will be an unforgettable afternoon for the Aussie striker.

9 July 2020
Leeds United v Stoke City, Championship

Having won the penalty that put Leeds 1-0 up against Stoke just before half-time, Hélder Costa scores the second himself to put the Whites firmly in control against the struggling Potters at Elland Road. Stuart Dallas's threaded pass into Costa's path sees the Angolan attempt a tricky turn – but when he realises he still has time, he toe-pokes past the keeper to make it 2-0.

48

28 May 1971
Juventus v Leeds United, Inter-Cities Fairs Cup Final, first leg

Paul Madeley equalises for United against Juventus in Turin in front of a partisan home crowd of almost 60,000. Trailing 1-0 at the Stadio Comunale, the Whites stun the Italians as Peter Lorimer wins the ball on the left flank before finding Madeley halfway inside the Juve half. Madeley is given too much time and space, which appears to make his mind up for him as he has time to size up a shot that takes a deflection and sneaks past the keeper to make it 1-1.

18 March 1972
Leeds United v Tottenham Hotspur, FA Cup quarter-final

Having levelled a minute before the break, United go 2-1 up against Spurs at Elland Road with a goal that will take Don Revie's men into the semi-final. Terry Cooper is fouled and the resulting free kick from Billy Bremner is powerfully headed home by Jack Charlton to put Leeds ahead.

19 August 1995
West Ham United v Leeds United, Premier League

Tony Yeboah starts the season as he means to go on as United level at Upton Park. Trailing to a fifth-minute goal from the Hammers, Leeds equalise when Gary Kelly swings in a fine cross from the right and

Yeboah arrives to head past the keeper from six yards to make it 1-1.

14 May 2009

Leeds United v Millwall, League One play-off semi-final, second leg

Jermaine Beckford misses a golden chance to put Leeds level on aggregate. Referee Mark Halsey spots a shirt pull by Andy Frampton on Sam Sodje as a Robert Snodgrass corner comes in and points to the spot. Initially, most of the near-38,000 Elland Road crowd think the official has awarded Millwall a free kick, but TV replays confirm the decision was correct. With 34 goals to his name already during the 2008/09 campaign, Beckford looks confident as he steps up, but his weak effort is easily saved by Millwall keeper David Forde, who also gets up to ensure Fabian Delph's follow-up goes wide to keep the score 0-0 and also ensure his side stay 1-0 up overall.

49

28 October 2003
Leeds United v Manchester United, League Cup third round

Roque Júnior puts Leeds ahead against Manchester United at Elland Road. After the first half of the tie ended goalless, the Brazilian powers a header past keeper Roy Carroll from Seth Johnson's cross to put Peter Reid's side 1-0 up.

4 May 2003
Arsenal v Leeds United, Premier League

Leeds go back in front away to Arsenal in the penultimate game of the 2002/03 campaign. Knowing a win will almost certainly guarantee Premier League survival, United are up for the battle at Highbury and, having scored inside the first five minutes of the first half, the Whites repeat the feat with a typically deadly free kick from Ian Harte, who curls a shot from 20 yards past David Seaman and into the bottom-left corner to put United 2-1 up. Incredibly, it is Harte's third goal in three visits to the Gunners' home ground.

29 November 2011
Nottingham Forest v Leeds United, Championship

United go 3-0 up at the City Ground with another fine goal against Nottingham Forest. The first two had been long-range efforts, but the third is a superb glancing header as Luciano Becchio's deft flick from an excellent left-wing cross by Michael Brown gives Forest keeper Lee Camp no chance, sending the Leeds fans behind the goal wild.

29 April 2017
Leeds United v Norwich City, Championship
An unlikely comeback looks on as United scramble a second goal in the space of five minutes against Norwich at Elland Road. As a corner is nodded down into the Canaries' six-yard box, the visitors fail to clear and Kyle Bartley manages to bundle the ball home from a yard out to reduce what had been a three-goal deficit to just one.

14 August 2021
Manchester United v Leeds United, Premier League
Luke Ayling's spectacular strike levels at Old Trafford. With Ayling having never previously scored a Premier League goal, when Stuart Dallas plays the ball to him 25 yards out, the home defenders are probably expecting him to look for another pass or maybe cross it into the box – so there is understandable surprise when he tees himself up and then fires a shot into the top-right corner, giving David de Gea no chance and making it 1-1. The Whites will, however, ship four more goals without reply on a miserable opening day to the 2021/22 campaign for Marcelo Bielsa's side.

50

27 January 2013
Leeds United v Tottenham Hotspur, FA Cup fourth round

Phrases such as 'giantkillers' or 'FA Cup shock' have generally been associated with teams facing Leeds, but as the years passed and the club remained absent from the top flight they came to be used about the Whites when they faced Premier League opposition. This is one of those occasions as Leeds take a 2-0 lead against Premier League Spurs at Elland Road. Ross McCormack is sent clear of the Spurs defence and as he gets into the box, he checks inside Stephen Caulker before curling a beautiful shot into the top-left corner of the net. The goal will be enough to see Neil Warnock's men through with an eventual 2-1 win, earning a place in the last 16 and a trip to face Manchester City at the Etihad Stadium.

13 August 2019
Salford City v Leeds United, League Cup first round

Hélder Costa claims a second assist as United go 2-0 up away to Salford. A simple set piece undoes the League Two side as Costa's near-post corner is headed home by Gaetano Berardi from a yard out to double the Whites' advantage at the Peninsula Stadium.

19 September 2020
Leeds United v Fulham, Premier League

United extend their lead over Fulham with a vital third goal just after the restart. Patrick Bamford had won the penalty that Mateusz Klich had then converted for the Whites' second goal and the roles are reversed on this occasion as Klich's precise through ball is taken on by Bamford, who calmly places an angled shot into the bottom-right corner to make it 3-1.

51

17 September 1969
Leeds United v Lyn, European Cup first round, first leg

United go 7-0 up against the beleaguered Norwegian champions and, just as with many of the previous goals, there is little the keeper can do to stop the onslaught as Billy Bremner taps a short free kick to his right and Johnny Giles thunders another superb shot into the top-left corner from 22 yards out for his second of the game.

26 May 1971
Juventus v Leeds United, Inter-Cities Fairs Cup Final, first leg

The referee, after consulting his linesmen, decides enough is enough and abandons the game in Turin due to torrential rain. With the score at 0-0, Billy Bremner argues strongly against the decision, but with the pitch waterlogged and no sign of the incessant rain stopping, the officials have no choice but to call a halt to proceedings.

22 September 1971
Barcelona v Leeds United, Inter-Cities Fairs Cup play-off

To signal the end of the Inter-Cities Fairs Cup as a European competition, the organisers arranged a one-off clash between the first winners, Barcelona, and the current holders and twice champions Leeds at the Camp Nou. The winner would get to keep the trophy permanently, with the UEFA Cup replacing it as one of Europe's three major tournaments. Though home advantage would ultimately sway the game the Catalans' way, United make a good fist of it and, after falling behind on 50 minutes, they level two minutes later. A typically thunderous Peter Lorimer free kick is pushed out by Barça keeper Salvador Sadurní and 19-year-old Joe Jordan – on his first start for the club – is first to the loose ball, turning in from close range to make it 1-1.

25 May 1987
Leeds United v Charlton Athletic, Second Division play-off final, second leg

Leeds' hopes of promotion back to the top flight get a huge boost when Brendan Ormsby scores to make it 1-0 at Elland Road. After defeat in the first leg to the Addicks at Crystal Palace's Selhurst Park, Ormsby's goal levels the aggregate at 1-1 – and though an untidy effort, none of the home support in the highly charged atmosphere care as Bob Taylor's determination sees his shot trickle towards the net where Ormsby makes absolutely certain as he taps it over the line to force a third game between the sides.

21 August 1995
Leeds United, v Liverpool, Premier League

A thunderous strike from the brilliant Tony Yeboah gives Leeds a 1-0 victory over Liverpool. The Ghanaian had already built up a cult following among the United supporters, but this goal takes everything to a new level as Tony Dorigo's chip to the edge of the Liverpool box finds Rod Wallace, who cleverly nods the ball back towards Yeboah. The striker hits an explosive volley from 25 yards that strikes the underside of the bar on its way into the roof of the net to send Elland Road into a mild state of hysteria.

4 April 2000
Leeds United v Deportivo La Coruña, Champions League quarter-final, first leg

United grab a deserved and crucial second goal up against Deportivo La Coruña. Olivier Dacourt, so impressive all night, feeds Harry Kewell on the left flank and the Australian digs out a superb cross that Alan Smith connects with at the near post to send a header downwards and past the keeper to put the Whites firmly in command at 2-0.

22 July 2020
Leeds United v Charlton Athletic, Championship

Pablo Hernández is directly involved for the third time as Leeds go 3-0 up against Charlton Athletic. The goal is a fairly simple affair, with Hernández floating a corner from the left toward the near post, where Tyler Roberts arrives unmarked to nod home unchallenged and seal a final-day victory for the champions.

52

23 January 2010
Tottenham Hotspur v Leeds United, FA Cup fourth round

Leeds scramble an equaliser at White Hart Lane to make it 1-1. After knocking out Manchester United in the previous round, a trip to north London represented another sizeable hurdle, but after going behind in the first half, the Whites level when a corner causes confusion in the Spurs defence. Jermaine Beckford somehow manages to hook the ball under the keeper to equalise.

53

6 May 1972
Leeds United v Arsenal, FA Cup Final

In a tough and combative final, Don Revie's United get the breakthrough in spectacular style against the Gunners. In a move that starts in the Leeds half, Peter Lorimer feeds Mick Jones on the right and he drives to the byline before sending a tempting cross into the box. It appears to have drifted too far away from goal until Allan Clarke arrives to meet the ball on the full and power it past keeper Geoff Barnett and into the bottom-left corner for what will be the only goal of the game. The 1-0 victory at Wembley is United's first FA Cup triumph and remains the only time the club has won the trophy.

14 May 2009
Leeds United v Millwall, League One play-off semi-final, second leg

Jermaine Beckford's penalty miss is quickly forgotten as Luciano Becchio gives United a 1-0 lead that levels the aggregate score at 1-1. The goal is the result of some superb play by left-back Ben Parker, who ushers a Millwall attack away from danger and then powers down the flank. After playing a short pass, he continues his run and receives the ball back before sliding a low cross into the six-yard box, where Becchio bundles home from close range to send a packed Elland Road wild.

6 March 2001
Real Madrid v Leeds United, Champions League second group stage

United level at the Bernabéu to make it 2-2 and set up a thrilling second half against Real Madrid. A set piece undoes the Spaniards' defence as Ian Harte's corner is nodded home by Mark Viduka with the Whites – whose kit was famously based on Real Madrid's by Don Revie – giving as good as they get in the Spanish capital.

5 April 2003
Charlton Athletic v Leeds United, Premier League

Mark Viduka grabs his second goal to put Leeds 4-1 up at Charlton in a game many believe the out-of-sorts Whites must win. In the bright south London sunshine, the Addicks are put to the sword as United show what they are capable of with Alan Smith – involved in every goal so far – claiming his third assist when nudging a pass to Viduka on the edge of the box as the Australian arrows a low shot into the bottom corner.

29 January 2017
Sutton United v Leeds United, FA Cup fourth round

A dark day for Leeds as James Collins strikes home the penalty that gives National League side Sutton a 1-0 victory. With 83 places between the teams in the pyramid, Garry Monk's side start as strong favourites, but the gamble of making ten changes backfires as Leeds exit the competition and record arguably their most embarrassing loss since the 3-2 defeat to Colchester United some 46 years earlier.

4 July 2020
Blackburn Rovers v Leeds United, Championship

Having seen a two-goal lead halved at Ewood Park, it takes Leeds just five minutes to restore their cushion. An attack sees the ball scrambled to the edge of the box where Mateusz Klich is waiting and his bobbling shot somehow beats the keeper to make it 3-1 with what will be the last goal of the game.

54

19 February 1972
Leeds United v Manchester United, First Division

Elland Road is rocking as Leeds go 2-0 up against Manchester United. Johnny Giles wins possession from Bobby Charlton and plays a fine pass out to Peter Lorimer arriving on the left flank. Lorimer moves past O'Neil and sends in a cross that Mick Jones hits on the volley past Alex Stepney, although the goal is later awarded to Allan Clarke who got the slightest of final touches.

11 February 1996
Birmingham City v Leeds United, League Cup semi-final, first leg

United grab a crucial equaliser at St Andrew's. Having fallen behind to Kevin Francis's first-half goal, Howard Wilkinson's side level when Tony Yeboah moves towards the Birmingham box, where former Leeds defender Chris Whyte allows the Ghanaian too much space and time and he drills a low shot through Whyte's legs and into the bottom-left corner from 18 yards.

25 February
Leeds United v Birmingham City, League Cup semi-final, second leg

United score nine minutes into the second half of the League Cup semi-final against Birmingham City – just as they had done in the first leg. Tony Yeboah fires a shot from 25 yards that is partially blocked, then the ball falls into the path of Gary McAllister in the box and his low shot is well saved, but Phil Masinga follows up to send a low shot under the keeper and put Leeds 1-0 up on the night and 3-1 ahead overall.

8 January 2011
Arsenal v Leeds United, FA Cup third round

Just a year after dumping Manchester United out of the FA Cup and holding Spurs away in the next round, Leeds threaten to take on the role of giantkillers again when they open up a shock lead away to Arsenal. With almost 9,000 travelling fans inside the Emirates, United go in front after Max Gradel is pulled down by Denílson in the box. Robert Snodgrass converts the penalty to put Leeds 1-0 up and only a late Cesc Fàbregas penalty will stop the Gunners from crashing out of the competition.

55

2 August 1969
Leeds United v Manchester City, FA Charity Shield
A well-worked moves ends with Leeds taking the lead in front of almost 40,000 Elland Road fans. Johnny Giles floats the ball in to the right of the City box where Billy Bremner nods it across to Eddie Gray, who is in acres of space, and the Scottish winger makes no mistake with a smart left-foot flick past goalkeeper Joe Corrigan to make it 1-0.

14 November 2002
Hapoel Tel Aviv v Leeds United, UEFA Cup second round, second leg
Alan Smith grabs his second goal of the game to put United in a strong position to progress in the UEFA Cup. It's something of a scrappy effort as Smith manages to get his head to the ball ahead of a couple of defenders, and it bobbles past the keeper for 2-1 on the night and 3-1 on aggregate in Israel.

11 May 2019
Derby County v Leeds United, Championship play-off semi-final, first leg
Kemar Roofe scores a crucial goal to give Leeds a 1-0 away victory at Pride Park. With what will be a sweet 16th of the campaign – and a fourth against Derby – Roofe smartly turns home Jack Harrison's left-wing cross to put his side

ahead after the Whites had stumbled badly on the run-In and missed out on automatic promotion.

23 October 2020
Aston Villa v Leeds United, Premier League

United break the deadlock away to Aston Villa with a poacher's goal from Patrick Bamford. Leeds attack down the left and Luke Ayling spots the run of Rodrigo and plays a short pass into his feet. Rodrigo gets into the box before firing an angled low drive in that the keeper parries, but Bamford is first to the loose ball, tucking it into the bottom-right corner of the net to make it 1-0 to Marcelo Bielsa's side.

56

17 March 1973
Leeds United v Rapid Bucharest, European Cup Winners' Cup quarter-final, first leg

Peter Lorimer strikes his second and United's fourth in a one-sided Cup Winners' Cup quarter-final at Elland Road. Rică Răducanu is again found wanting as Lorimer tries his luck from 25 yards and his shot flies past the keeper and into the net to make it 4-0 on the night and place one Leeds foot firmly into the semi-finals.

25 February
Leeds United v Birmingham City, League Cup semi-final, second leg

A second goal in the space of three second-half minutes virtually secures a place in the League Cup Final for Leeds, who go 2-0 up against the First Division side. Gary Kelly's ball into the Birmingham box is headed upwards by Brian Deane, who then nods it again, this time towards Tony Yeboah. The Ghanaian launches himself into a spectacular acrobatic kick that goes in off the right-hand post to make it 4-1 on aggregate.

5 April 2003
Charlton Athletic v Leeds United, Premier League

Having argued over the first penalty, Mark Viduka and Ian Harte are in agreement that the Aussie should have the chance to complete his hat-trick when United win a second spot-kick at The Valley. Alan Smith – who had made three goals and already won one penalty – is again sent sprawling in the box, this time by Charlton's Luke Young, and Viduka calmly sends the keeper the wrong way to make it 5-1 and secure the match ball in the process.

8 May 2006
Preston North End v Leeds United, Championship play-off semi-final, second leg

United get a vital goal to go 1-0 up against Preston at Deepdale and lead 2-1 on aggregate. Having been held 1-1 at Elland Road, the Whites travelled over the Pennines as slight underdogs to progress to the final, but Gary Kelly's corner is glanced home by Rob Hulse to swing the momentum back in Kevin Blackwell's side's favour. It is the first goal North End have conceded at home in more than nine hours.

27 June May 2020
Leeds United v Fulham, Championship

United double their lead against Fulham at Elland Road. Jack Harrison races down the right before sending a low ball into the box. It is missed by a succession of Fulham defenders before falling to Ezgjan Alioski, who takes a touch to control before planting his shot into the bottom-right corner to wrong-foot the keeper and put Leeds 2-0 up.

19 July 2020
Derby County v Leeds United, Championship

Champions Leeds level at Pride Park, having fallen behind just two minutes before. Pablo Hernández starts the move that leads to the equaliser as he sprays a ball out to the right of the Derby box, but it is played back to him. The elegant Spaniard's first shot is half-cleared, but his second attempt is a rising shot past the keeper from 18 yards to make it 1-1.

57

19 August 1995
West Ham United v Leeds United, Premier League

Leeds go ahead against West Ham at Upton Park with a typically spectacular goal from crowd idol Tony Yeboah. The Ghanaian had joined the Whites the previous January and quickly become a huge favourite with the fans – his second on the opening day of the 1995/96 campaign underlines why as he runs on to Gary Kelly's delightful chip before thundering an angled volley into the roof of the net for Howard Wilkinson's side to secure an opening-day 2-1 win.

5 August 2018
Leeds United v Stoke City, Championship

Leeds restore their two-goal advantage over Stoke via a set piece. The Potters – fresh from relegation from the Premier League – had halved the deficit just five minutes earlier from the penalty spot, but any hopes they have of turning the game on its head are dented when Barry Douglas whips in a corner that Liam Cooper meets with a downward header across Jack Butland and into the bottom-left corner to make it 3-1 and ensure that the Marcelo Bielsa era starts with a victory.

19 September 2020
Leeds United v Fulham, Premier League

Leeds look set for a big win in the first home match of the 2020/21 campaign as Hélder Costa makes it 4-1 against

Fulham with an hour not yet played. Patrick Bamford had been involved in the previous two goals and he is again on this occasion as his excellent low cross from the left finds the unmarked Costa, who hits an unstoppable left-foot drive into the top-left corner from ten yards. With the Cottagers later pulling two goals back and hitting the post in the time that remains, it proves to be a crucial strike.

9 July 2020
Leeds United v Stoke City, Championship

Stoke are again undone by the slick passing of Leeds as they fall further behind at Elland Road. Jack Harrison plays a smart pass inside a full-back to get Pablo Hernández in behind the Potters' defence. The Spaniard then picks out Liam Cooper in the middle and his shot kisses the right-hand post before flying into the opposite corner of the net to make it 3-0.

58

2 August 1969
Leeds United v Manchester City, FA Charity Shield

A second goal in the space of four minutes puts the Whites firmly in command at Elland Road. Just as had been the case with the opening goal, Johnny Giles is the architect as he floats a tempting cross into the box for Jack Charlton to leap above his marker and direct a header into the far corner of the net, giving Joe Corrigan no chance. It will effectively win Leeds' first Charity Shield, despite a late consolation goal for City's Colin Bell.

19 February 1972
Leeds United v Manchester United, First Division

Having seen a 2-0 lead halved a minute before, Leeds respond immediately to restore their advantage against Manchester United at an electric and packed-out Elland Road. Out on the right, Billy Bremner takes on Tony Dunne and beats him comfortably before sending a tempting cross towards the back post, where Mick Jones thumps a header downwards and past Reds keeper Alex Stepney to make it 3-1.

13 August 2019
Salford City v Leeds United, League Cup first round

A third Leeds goal in the space of 15 minutes puts the tie firmly to bed as United make it 3-0 away to Salford City. It's the best goal of the night, too, as Mateusz Klich collects a ball out of defence just over the halfway line and drives towards goal. Eddie Nketiah makes an intelligent decoy run to his right, but Klich has only one thing in mind as he cuts inside and then fires a beauty into the top-right corner from 20 yards to end the contest and ensure the Whites' first trip to the Peninsula Stadium is a happy one.

Another day, another goal of the season for Tony Yeboah – this time against Wimbledon in September 1995

Spectacular goal-machine Tony Yeboah in action versus Sheffield Wednesday (January 1995)

(Left) Billy Bremner in action in the 1970 FA Cup Final replay against Chelsea. Ron 'Chopper' Harris heads the ball clear from in front of Jack Charlton

Johnny Giles and Norman Hunter celebrate a goal against Crystal Palace in 1972

Jack Charlton in action v Stoke (1972)

Peter Lorimer scores against Chelsea in 1967

Mick Jones (floor) scores against Liverpool as Billy Bremner watches on (October 1972)

Harry Kewell on target against Southampton (December 2002)

Mark Viduka grabs United's second goal against Liverpool (February 2004)

Allan Clarke celebrates with Peter Lorimer (October 1972)

Patrick Bamford scores during a 5-2 win over Newcastle United at Elland Road (December 2020)

Stuart Dallas scores the first of two goals away to Manchester City (April 2021)

Johnny Giles in action against Everton (February 1972)

Billy Bremner walks off the pitch having been sent for an early bath after his infamous FA Charity Shield altercation with Liverpool's Kevin Keegan.

Rod Wallace scores the winner against Norwich for First Division champions Leeds (May 1992)

59

8 May 2010
Leeds United v Bristol Rovers, League One

With nails being bitten to the bone and ten-man United 1-0 down, Elland Road – packed to capacity on a day when automatic promotion is expected – erupts just before the hour. With a palpable sense of injustice among the Leeds players and supporters following Max Gradel's first-half dismissal, sub Jonny Howson scores a beauty as Luciano Becchio lays the ball off for the youngster and his curling effort from 20 yards beats the keeper to make it 1-1 and set up a thrilling final half-hour.

3 October 2020
Leeds United v Manchester City, Premier League

Trailing 1-0 in a fast and entertaining clash with Manchester City, United get a deserved equaliser. Raheem Sterling had given the visitors a 17th-minute lead, but the Whites level just before the hour as a corner is fumbled by Brazilian keeper Ederson, leaving Rodrigo with the simplest of tap-ins to make it 1-1 and earn his side a point.

60

7 October 1967
Leeds United v Chelsea, First Division

The 40,460 Elland Road crowd continues to lap up a display of supreme attacking football and dominance as Eddie Gray makes it 5-0 against Chelsea. Jimmy Greenhoff cuts inside from the right before teeing up Gray who lashes a shot past Peter Bonetti from 20 yards.

28 November 1970
Leeds United v Manchester City, First Division

United grab what will be the only goal of the game against City at Elland Road with an hour played. Peter Lorimer refuses to give up on a ball that looks to be going out for a goal kick and catches the City defence napping as he manages to send a square pass to Allan Clarke, who makes no mistake from inside the box to give the Whites a 1-0 victory.

3 March 1972
Leeds United v Southampton, First Division

Leeds' incessant pressure pays off against Southampton with the third of seven goals at Elland Road. Billy Bremner feeds Eddie Gray down the middle with a clever disguised pass, and the Scotland winger spots Alan Clarke free on the left of the box. Clarke expertly sidesteps a defender before sending an angled low drive into the bottom-left corner of the net.

10 August 1974
Liverpool v Leeds United, FA Charity Shield

In a game meant to be a showpiece friendly and little more, both teams are penalised for a series of violent clashes. Johnny Giles appears to throw a punch at Kevin Keegan to begin with and the Liverpool player goes down clutching his face. Moments later, Billy Bremner – who had been the subject of a rash Keegan tackle shortly beforehand – appears to exchange punches with the fired-up Liverpool star and both are dismissed as a result. It was hardly the way new manager Brian Clough had wanted to begin his tenure as Leeds boss and the FA will later ban Bremner for several weeks in a game remembered for all the wrong reasons.

11 August 2018
Derby County v Leeds United, Championship

A superb second goal for Kemar Roofe puts Leeds 3-1 up at Pride Park. Kalvin Phillips wins possession back midway inside the Rams' half and feeds Mateusz Klich. He plays a short pass to Roofe's feet and, with his back to goal, he spins away from two defenders to give himself room to rifle a powerful left-foot drive into the top-left corner, giving keeper Scott Carson no chance.

61

17 September 1969
Leeds United v Lyn, European Cup first round, first leg

Mick Jones grabs his hat-trick as Leeds go 8-0 up against the Norwegians. Jones powers into the box before dragging a low shot that strikes the foot of the left-hand post and rebounds across goal and into the opposite corner of the net to leave the punch-drunk visitors still 29 minutes from the final whistle and facing a cricket score.

14 April 1971
Liverpool v Leeds United, Inter-Cities Fairs Cup semi-final first leg

Billy Bremner grabs a vital away goal as Leeds look to take an advantage back to Elland Road. At a misty and packed Anfield, United had defended comfortably and look to open the scoring when a free kick is awarded out on the left flank. The Liverpool defence line up for the cross into the box, but as Johnny Giles floats in the ball, the Reds neglect to mark Bremner who rises to power a header past Ray Clemence and into the bottom-right corner of the net to silence the Kop and secure a superb 1-0 victory on Merseyside.

8 May 2006
Preston North End v Leeds United, Championship play-off semi-final, second leg

A second goal in the space of five minutes knocks the stuffing out of Preston and puts United in firm control.

Liam Miller finds Rob Hulse, who drives into the box and whips in a low cross that Frazer Richardson meets at the far post to squeeze his shot beneath keeper Carlo Nash for 2-0 on the night, and 3-1 on aggregate, at Deepdale. It will be enough to send the Whites into the final at the Millennium Stadium in Cardiff where Watford await, with promotion to the Premier League the prize for the winners.

16 December 2020

Leeds United v Newcastle United, Premier League

A superb goal puts Leeds 2-1 up against Newcastle at Elland Road. Having earlier trailed 1-0, United get their noses in front when Rodrigo controls a pass 35 yards out before playing it left for Jack Harrison. The on-loan Manchester City star does well to bring a high ball down and then pings it to the edge of the box, where Rodrigo arrives to direct a diving header into the bottom-right corner from 12 yards out to give the Whites a deserved lead. It was a fantastic cross and an even better header.

62

19 February 1972
Leeds United v Manchester United, First Division

Leeds continue to dismantle a poor Manchester United side with a fourth goal in 15 second-half minutes. Again, it's all too easy for the Whites as Eddie Gray dances past Tony Dunne before picking out Peter Lorimer on the right of the box. The Scot's low cross finds Mick Jones, who taps home from a yard or so out to make it 4-1.

28 May 1975
Bayern Munich v Leeds United, European Cup Final

There's moment that still sticks in the craw of Leeds fans when the feeling of injustice reaches fever pitch. Having already been denied a blatant penalty after Franz Beckenbauer tripped Allan Clarke, who seemed set to score the opening goal, Whites fans and their players are incandescent with rage as a goal that would have made it 1-0 is disallowed. A ball comes into the Bayern box and is headed partially clear, but only as far as Peter Lorimer who lashes a volley past keeper Sepp Maier from eight yards and into the net. The referee initially seems to signal a goal until the wily Beckenbauer protests long enough for the official to double check with the linesman. The end result is that Billy Bremner is adjudged to have been offside, but if he was, it is so marginal as to seem impossible to call accurately and, as he didn't interfere with the shot or the keeper's line of view, it is an incredibly harsh decision. With numerous other calls going against

Leeds during the game – and given the controversies in
the European Cup Winners' Cup Final loss to AC Milan
a couple of years before – it is the final straw for many
United fans as unrest breaks out around the stadium.
Munich go on to win 2-0, but is a game nobody from
Elland Road will forget, for all the wrong reasons.

29 December 2010
Leeds United v Portsmouth, Championship
Leeds regain their two-goal cushion over a resilient and
hard-working Portsmouth in a thrilling Championship
clash at Elland Road. Pompey keeper Jamie Ashdown
keeps Max Gradel's header out for a corner, but when
Robert Snodgrass's delivery isn't cleared, Bradley Johnson
fires in a low shot to make it 3-1. Bizarrely, Andy O'Brien
will score two own goals to give Pompey a share of the
spoils and a 3-3 draw that robs United of the two points
that would have sent them into second spot.

15 May 2019
Leeds United v Derby County, Championship play-off semi-final, second leg
Elland Road erupts as Stuart Dallas scores to make it 3-2
in Derby's favour on the night but 3-3 on aggregate. As
the Whites battle to stay in contention for the play-off final
and ensure they aren't the first club to lose a semi having
won the away leg first, Dallas buries a low curling shot
into the bottom-right corner of the net after running on to
Mateusz Klich's ball and cutting in from the left. Sadly, it
won't be enough as the Rams grab a dramatic late fourth
to set up a final against Aston Villa at Wembley.

63

14 March 2001
Leeds United v Lazio, Champions League second group stage

United, already assured of a quarter-final spot, go 3-2 up against Lazio in an entertaining final group stage clash at Elland Road. As ever, the Whites' devastating full-backs are involved again as Ian Harte matches Gary Kelly's earlier assist with a cross that Mark Viduka muscles his way to powering home a header in a game that will eventually end 3-3.

14 November 2002
Hapoel Tel Aviv v Leeds United, UEFA Cup second round, second leg

Alan Smith completes his hat-trick to make it 3-1 on the night and 4-1 on aggregate. Smith's treble comes when he meets Harry Kewell's cross with a thumping header and, though keeper Shavit Elimelech makes a fine save, Smith smashes home the rebound to ensure he travels back from Israel with the match ball.

8 May 2010
Leeds United v Bristol Rovers, League One

Elland Road explodes as ten-man Leeds go 2-1 up in a bad-tempered promotion decider. Victory would send Leeds back to the Championship, but having had Max Gradel sent off and then falling behind just after the restart, things seems to be going badly wrong. Jonny Howson's leveller on 59 saw the belief surge back and when keeper Mikkel Andersen's throw is intercepted by Jermaine Beckford, the striker plays it left to Bradley Johnson, who moves into the box and although his cross-shot is blocked by a Rovers defender, the ball is presented to Beckford who forces it home from six yards to make it 2-1 – a goal that will be enough to win the game and clinch automatic promotion as League One runners-up.

64

15 April 1972
Leeds United v Birmingham City, FA Cup semi-final

United fans begin to celebrate victory with just over an hour played at Hillsborough. The elegant Johnny Giles races clear of his marker on the right before sending a cross over keeper Paul Cooper and on to the chest of Mick Jones, who guides the ball into the empty net to make it 3-0 and set the Whites on the way to a Wembley showdown with Arsenal.

3 March 1972
Leeds United v Southampton, First Division

Southampton fail to clear a free kick and pay the price as Billy Bremner wins possession back for Johnny Giles and, although he is fouled as the ball comes to him, the referee waves play on and Peter Lorimer collects the loose ball and drives it across the keeper. A despairing Saints defender can only help the ball into his own net to make it 4-0 at Elland Road.

12 September 1995
AS Monaco v Leeds United, UEFA Cup first round, first leg

A quite brilliant goal from a striker at the very top of his game and yet another spectacular effort to add to the ever-increasing Tony Yeboah collection. There seems little danger when the Ghanaian picks up the ball on the right of the AS Monaco box, but he spins off his marker before hitting a sumptuous curling effort into the top-left corner to put Leeds 2-0 up against the French side. It is both instinctive and brilliant from Yeboah, who can do no wrong in the eyes of the United fans.

27 February 1996
Port Vale v Leeds United, FA Cup fifth round replay

United finally draw level with a determined and resolute Port Vale at Vale Park. The second-tier Potteries side had held the Whites to a 0-0 draw at Elland Road and initially took command of the replay, going in front during the first half, but midway through the second half Gary McAllister levels. Tomas Brolin manages to dig a cross out from the left and McAllister rises to nod the ball into the bottom-left corner to make it 1-1 with a rare headed goal and set up a thrilling last quarter.

17 January 2006
Leeds United v Wigan Athletic, FA Cup third round replay

United peg back Premier League Wigan for the second time at Elland Road. The first equaliser had come via a corner kick and another corner results in an opportunity for David Healy, as the threat of Rob Hulse causes Matt Jackson to handle the ball and the referee points to the spot. Healy confidently tucks home to make it 2-2 with his second of the match.

11 August 2018
Derby County v Leeds United, Championship

United fans are starting to get excited about the Marcelo Bielsa era as a ruthless Leeds go 4-1 up away to Frank

Lampard's Derby. The killer fourth – and final goal of the game – comes when a long ball from the Leeds half looks to be heading out of play for a goal kick until Pablo Hernández somehow keeps it in and crosses into the middle for Ezgjan Alioski to head powerfully into the middle of the goal with Scott Carson unable to stop the ball despite getting a hand to it.

65

28 April 1962
Newcastle United v Leeds United, Second Division

Albert Johanneson repays strike partner Billy McAdams as he assists Leeds' second goal at St James' Park. McAdams had set up Johanneson's opener and it is from his cross that McAdams profits as the keeper fails to catch cleanly and the relegation-threatened Whites go 2-0 up.

17 April 1968
Leeds United v Tottenham Hotspur, First Division

With Don Revie's side chasing an unprecedented quadruple of trophies, victory over Spurs at Elland Road was crucial in the final weeks of an unforgettable campaign for United. In what was the 58th game of the season, the Whites – already winners of the League Cup – were also in the semi-finals of the FA Cup and Inter-Cities Fairs Cup. Victory over Spurs would leave Leeds a point behind leaders Manchester United with a game in hand, and victory comes in controversial circumstances as the referee points to the spot when keeper Pat Jennings clatters into Mick Jones in the box. Peter Lorimer thumps the penalty home to secure a 1-0 win, with Spurs furious at the decision.

17 September 1969
Leeds United v Lyn, European Cup first round, first leg

United make it nine against Lyn with Billy Bremner – involved in several of the first eight goals – finally getting on the scoresheet as the diminutive Scot plays a smart one-two with Terry Cooper before drilling a low angled shot just inside the left upright.

17 March 1973
Leeds United v Rapid Bucharest, European Cup Winners' Cup quarter-final, first leg

Joe Jordan wraps up a fine first-leg win over Rapid as the Whites declare at five at Elland Road. Paul Madeley finds Allan Clarke, who carries the ball more than 20 yards towards goal before teeing up Jordan, who drives home inside the box to complete the rout and make it 5-0. United will win the second leg 3-1 in Romania to progress to the semi-finals, where Yugoslavian giants Hajduk Split await Don Revie's men.

9 May 1973
Leeds United v Arsenal, First Division

Leeds go 3-1 up against Arsenal as Peter Lorimer completes a memorable hat-trick at Elland Road. Having seen a two-goal lead halved just after the restart, the Whites re-establish their cushion over the Gunners when Joe Jordan finds Lorimer, who makes no mistake with a typically assured and lethal finish as Leeds look to end their league campaign on a high ahead of the European Cup Winners' Cup Final against AC Milan.

26 April 1992
Sheffield United v Leeds United, First Division

When David Batty is chopped down on the left of the Blades' box, it gives Leeds the chance to try and go ahead for the first time in this crucial Yorkshire derby. Having fallen behind, levelled and then struck the post, it's no surprise when Gary McAllister sends the perfect cross towards the far post and as keeper Mel Rees – still injured from a collision earlier in the game – badly misjudges the flight, Jon Newsome heads home into the empty net to edge the Whites towards the First Division title.

13 April 2019
Leeds United v Sheffield Wednesday, Championship

Jack Harrison scores the only goal of the Yorkshire derby with Sheffield Wednesday at Elland Road to leave United needing ten points from their final four matches to secure promotion to the Premier League. In a tense game, the winner comes when Pablo Hernández sends a low ball into the Owls' box and Harrison sweeps a deft low shot past the keeper and into the bottom-left corner to secure a vital three points for Marcelo Bielsa's men.

66

9 January 2000
Manchester City v Leeds United, FA Cup third round

Lee Bowyer's superb half-volley at last gives United daylight against second-tier Manchester City. In what is an absorbing FA Cup tie, Jason Wilcox is sent clear on the left and his clever cross picks out the unmarked Bowyer in the City box. His first-time shot from ten yards arrows into the top-left-hand corner like a bullet to make it 4-2 – a quite sublime finish by the United midfielder.

4 April 2000
Leeds United v Deportivo La Coruña, Champions League quarter-final, first leg

Rio Ferdinand scores to put Leeds within sight of a Champions League semi-final. With the Spanish side on the ropes in the first leg at Elland Road, a Harry Kewell corner is deflected across the six-yard box and Ferdinand thumps a header past the desperate efforts of the Deportivo defenders and into the net for his first goal for the club, making the score 3-0.

14 September 2002
Lees United v Manchester United, Premier League

Terry Venables' Leeds grab what will be the only goal of the game against Manchester United to send Elland Road crazy. Ian Harte out-foxes Luke Chadwick, who is lulled into thinking he had won the duel with the Whites' left-back as he prevents him from crossing on his favoured foot – but Harte simply checks in on his right and sends in an equally effective ball into the box where Harry Kewell leaps to plant a header past Fabien Barthez and into the far corner of the Red Devils' net.

29 November 2011
Nottingham Forest v Leeds United, Championship

United wrap up a fitting tribute to the legendary Gary Speed, who had tragically died just two days before, with a fourth goal against Nottingham Forest at the City Ground. Jonny Howson drives into the Forest box with a mazy run but is denied by keeper Lee Camp, although Adam Clayton wants the loose ball more than anyone else and hammers a high shot home from six yards to complete a 4-0 win.

22 July 2020
Leeds United v Charlton Athletic, Championship

Jamie Shackleton provides the icing on the cake as champions Leeds complete a 4-0 win over Charlton. Ian Poveda is the provider, bursting down the right and into the box before squaring a simple pass into the path of Shackleton, who expertly sweeps a low shot into the bottom-left corner and gives the keeper no chance. The win confirms that Charlton – managed by former United star Lee Bowyer – are relegated to the third tier and, as a result, this will be Bowyer's last game in charge.

12 September 2020
Liverpool v Leeds United, Premier League

Leeds stun champions Liverpool with a third equaliser at Anfield to make it 3-3 in an opening-day classic at Anfield. Each time the champions had gone ahead, the Whites had responded in kind and Mateusz Klich brings his side level as he receives the ball on the right of the Reds' box before whipping a shot across Alisson and into the bottom-left corner. Though Marcelo Bielsa's side eventually lose 4-3, it is a proud day for all United fans as the club announce their return to the top flight in thrilling fashion.

67

20 April 2000
Leeds United v Galatasaray, UEFA Cup semi-final, second leg

United level on the night against Galatasary but still need three more in the time that remains to see off the Turks at Elland Road. After Brazilian keeper Cláudio Taffarel makes a fine save to keep out a miscued clearance on 66 minutes, the Whites win a corner and Eirik Bakke rises above everyone to head home his second of the night and make it 2-2. But with the visitors 4-2 up overall, it proves too much of a task to turn around for David O'Leary's men with no further scoring.

28 December 2009
Stockport County v Leeds United, League One

League One table-toppers Leeds had been stunned by basement side Stockport County at Edgeley Park where the hosts – who had lost their last ten games – led 2-1. But Simon Grayson's side finally find a way back into the game midway through the second period when Patrick Kisnorbo's excellent cross into the box finds Jermaine Beckford, who heads home to make it 2-2 and set up a thrilling finish against the Greater Manchester side.

27 August 2019
Leeds United v Stoke City, League Cup second round

Eddie Nketiah pulls a goal back as Leeds look to avoid a defeat by Stoke in the League Cup. The visitors had gone in 2-0 up at the break at Elland Road and had survived half of the second period when Nketiah, on loan from Arsenal, strikes. Jack Butland's poor goal kick hits one of his own players 40 yards from goal and bounces back to Nketiah, who hadn't moved back upfield, so he gratefully accepts the gift, nutmegging Butland before slotting into the empty net to halve the deficit.

23 October 2020
Aston Villa v Leeds United, Premier League

The Whites double their advantage away to Aston Villa with a stunning Patrick Bamford goal. There seems little on for the forward as he receives a pass on the edge of the Villa box, but he works himself a yard of space, looks up and then strikes a left-foot shot into the top-left corner from 20 yards with an effort that swerves this way and that en route to the back of the net. The keeper has no chance and Bamford suddenly has two goals inside 12 minutes with Leeds now 2-0 up.

68

3 March 1972
Leeds United v Southampton, First Division

Awful defending by Southampton leads to goal number five for Leeds. The visitors had been abject all afternoon and the fifth goal is typical of their display as Fry's loose pass is collected by Peter Lorimer, who has one thing in his mind as he drives a low shot past the keeper and into the bottom-left corner to complete his hat-trick.

7 May 2011
Queens Park Rangers v Leeds United, Championship

Needing a win to keep hopes alive of sneaking into the play-offs on the final day, Leeds go 2-1 up against champions QPR at Loftus Road. What proves to be the winning goal comes when Ross McCormack surges into the Rangers box before seeing his shot deflect off QPR's Kaspars Gorkšs on its way into the net to give United a 2-1 win. However, Nottingham Forest's victory away to Crystal Palace means they and not the Whites take the last play-off spot.

29 December 2019
Birmingham City v Leeds United, Championship

Games between Leeds and Birmingham have rarely been dull over the years and this clash continues that tradition as United go back in front at St Andrew's. After trailing 2-0, the Blues had pegged back Marcelo Bielsa's promotion-chasing Whites, but a rare Luke Ayling strike makes it 3-2 as he cuts inside from the right flank, moving away from Jérémie Bela, and with nobody closing him down he strikes a half-volley, just inside the left post.

69

6 April 1974
Leeds United v Derby County, First Division

United get the crucial second goal against Derby in a top-of-the-table clash at Elland Road. Trevor Cherry floats a free kick into the Rams' box where David Nish out-jumps Joe Jordan to clear the danger, but only as far as the unmarked Billy Bremner, who watches the ball carefully before sending a low, right-foot volley that has enough power to beat the keeper and seal what will be a fine victory that keeps hopes of another title success alive.

23 May 2021
Leeds United v West Bromwich Albion, Premier League

Gaetano Berardi bids an emotional farewell to the 8,000 Leeds United fans allowed in Elland Road as he is substituted on his last appearance for the club. The popular Swiss defender had spent seven years with the Whites, clocking up 157 appearances along the way.

70

7 April 1973
Leeds United v Wolverhampton Wanderers, FA Cup semi-final

Leeds book a place in the final with a narrow 1-0 win over Wolves at Manchester City's Maine Road. The only goal of the game comes when a United corner from the left is cleared out of the box, but it is hooked back in towards Mick Jones and, as a defender gets a touch, the ball falls kindly for Billy Bremner, who drives it into the net via the keeper's attempted save to send the Whites back to Wembley, where Second Division Sunderland await.

10 August 1974
Liverpool v Leeds United, FA Charity Shield

Trevor Cherry's superb header makes it 1-1 against Liverpool at Wembley. In a game littered with bad tackles, violence and ill temper, Cherry's goal is a thing of beauty as Peter Lorimer skips past a challenge midway inside the Liverpool half before sending a lofted ball towards the six-yard box, where Cherry out-jumps his marker to gently guide a header past Ray Clemence and finally give the Leeds fans something to cheer about.

20 April 1974
Leeds United v Ipswich Town, First Division

Having been pegged back from 2-0 up to 2-2, Leeds hang on against Bobby Robson's determined Ipswich Town.

But with the chance to be crowned champions of England within touching distance, United dig deep to score the fifth and decisive goal of the game. Paul Reaney's cross is flicked on by Peter Lorimer into the path of Allan Clarke who controls the ball before thumping a shot past Paul Cooper to make it 3-2 and seal the two points that will prove crucial for Don Revie's side in clinching the First Division title.

9 April 1975
Barcelona v Leeds United, European Cup semi-final, second leg

It all looks to be going horribly wrong in Europe yet again for this talented Leeds United side as a 1-0 lead and 3-1 aggregate advantage suddenly becomes 1-1 on the night and 3-2 overall and, moments later, United are reduced to ten men. With the 110,000 crowd baying for Barça to go and get a second, a long ball is played forward and as Gordon McQueen challenges for a header, he loses his cool after the ball is cleared and swings a punch at the Barcelona man. The referee has spotted it and issues a straight red to McQueen. With 20 minutes remaining, it seems the Catalan side will go and win the game and book a place in the final, but despite several near misses for the hosts, the Whites hang on to claim a famous 1-1 draw and progress to the final where Bayern Munich await them in Paris.

23 April 1977
Leeds United v Manchester United, FA Cup semi-final

After trailing 2-0 inside the first 15 minutes, Leeds have a chance to halve the deficit when Joe Jordan is pulled down in the box and the referee awards a penalty. Allan Clarke steps up to take the spot-kick at the end most of the Red Devils' fans are housed and tucks a low shot to the left of Alex Stepney, who gets a hand to the ball but can't prevent it crossing the line to make it 2-1 at Hillsborough.

25 September 2012
Leeds United v Everton, League Cup third round

United grab what will prove to be the killer goal against a much-changed Premier League Everton. Rodolph Austin is fouled by Séamus Coleman on the left flank and El Hadji Diouf plays a short ball to the edge of the Toffees' box for Danny Pugh to have a crack at goal. As his shot bobbles goalwards, the lively Austin gets a touch that takes it past defenders and the keeper and into the net to make it 2-0 – a scoreline that will ease the Championship Whites into round four.

23 May 2021
Leeds United v West Bromwich Albion, Premier League

After five wonderful years as a Leeds United player, Pablo Hernández waves goodbye to the fans who idolise him as he is subbed for the final time. The graceful Spaniard had been much-travelled before arriving at Elland Road, and he made 175 appearances for the Whites over a five-year period, scoring 36 goals.

31 January 2021
Leicester City v Leeds United, Premier League

Leeds go ahead against Leicester for the first time at the King Power Stadium with another slick goal. The Whites' movement is excellent and, when Raphinha's quick pass spins into the feet of Patrick Bamford, he gets his body around the ball before turning and hooking a shot into the top-right corner, giving Kasper Schmeichel no chance and making it 2-1.

71

19 November 2005
Southampton v Leeds United, Championship

After going in 3-0 down to Southampton at St Mary's, Leeds begin a fightback that will stun the hosts. With less than 20 minutes remaining, Gary Kelly's corner on the right finds the head of Paul Butler and the skipper's header beats a defender on the line to reduce the arrears to just a couple of goals.

27 June 2020
Leeds United v Fulham, Championship

United complete a convincing victory over promotion rivals Fulham at Elland Road with a third goal. United go direct and catch the Cottagers on the back foot as Pablo Hernández lofts a superb pass into the path of Jack Harrison, who runs on to the ball before squeezing a low shot past the keeper from a tight angle to wrap up a 3-0 win and send Leeds back to the top of the table.

72

11 February 1996
Birmingham City v Leeds United, League Cup semi-final first leg

Former United defender Chris Whyte's day goes from bad to worse as he gets the final touch on a Tony Yeboah header to put Leeds 2-1 up at St Andrew's. Gary Kelly chases a seemingly lost cause into the corner and digs out a cross for Yeboah, near the penalty spot, to head down and, as the ball bounces up, Whyte inadvertently helps it over his own keeper to put the Whites firmly in the box seat.

9 July 2020
Leeds United v Stoke City, Championship

Game, set and match for the Championship leaders who continue to pummel Stoke at Elland Road. Luke Ayling sends Hélder Costa away down the right flank and his low cross is dummied by Patrick Bamford for Pablo Hernández to curl home a low drive from the edge of the box and make it 4-0.

29 December 2020
West Bromwich Albion v Leeds United, Premier League

Raphinha wraps up Leeds' joint biggest away winning margin in the club's history as he makes it 5-0 against West Brom. It's yet another superb goal from the Brazilian as he is fed on the left by Stuart Dallas before cutting in towards the edge of the Baggies' box and unleashing a powerful left foot-drive into the top corner.

21 August 2021
Leeds United v Everton, Premier League

United come from behind for the second time to earn a 2-2 draw with Everton in an entertaining opening-day clash at Elland Road. It's a goal straight out of the top drawer, too, as a cross from the left comes in and as the ball drops to the ground, Liam Cooper tees up Raphinha who strikes an angled bullet of a shot into the bottom-left corner to once again send a feverish Elland Road wild. A superb goal from the Brazilian.

73

3 March 1972
Leeds United v Southampton, First Division

United go 6-0 up against Southampton at Elland Road and it's a goal created and scored by centre-backs Norman Hunter and Jack Charlton. With the game won long before, the defenders decide to get in on the act and join the attack. When the ball is fed to Hunter on the left wing, his excellent cross into the Saints box is headed home by Charlton as the Whites continue to thrill and delight in equal measure.

23 September 1995
Wimbledon v Leeds United, Premier League

United end any hopes of a Wimbledon revival with a fourth goal of the afternoon at Selhurst Park. The Dons had stoically refused to give up at their temporary home of Selhurst Park, but Phil Masinga's goal will be the final nail in the coffin. The South African runs down the right flank before cutting inside and into the box where he tees up Tony Yeboah to sweep home a low, right-foot shot into the bottom-right corner to complete his hat-trick, making it 4-2 for Howard Wilkinson's men and sealing the three points.

24 December 1995
Leeds United v Manchester United, Premier League

Brian Deane gets the vital third goal that ensures all Leeds fans have a perfect Christmas. Carlton Palmer gets into the Red Devils' penalty area on the right before checking back and playing a short pass to Tomas Brolin. The Swede's lofted ball flies towards the six-yard box, where Deane leaps to head past Peter Schmeichel and seal a 3-1 victory at Elland Road.

4 November 2000
Leeds United v Liverpool, Premier League
A stunning individual goal by Mark Viduka brings Leeds level yet again in a rollercoaster of a game with Liverpool at Elland Road. Olivier Dacourt plays a short pass to the Australian's feet on the edge of the Liverpool box and, taking the ball in his stride, Viduka has the nous to stop, back-heel himself around a defender to create enough space to place a low shot across the keeper and into the bottom-left corner. This completes his hat-trick and makes it 3-3, setting up a grandstand finish in the process.

18 May 2021
Southampton v Leeds United, Premier League
United's slender hopes of a top-six finish get a huge boost when Patrick Bamford bags his 16th Premier League goal of a superb season for the much-travelled striker at St Mary's. The game seems to be heading for a 0-0 draw when Rodrigo's superb chip finds Bamford in behind the Saints defence and he manages to squeeze a deft shot through keeper Alex McCarthy's legs to make it 1-0 for the Whites.

74

19 February 1972
Leeds United v Manchester United, First Division

Leeds wrap up a satisfying 5-1 win over Manchester United at Elland Road with a fifth goal in just 27 minutes. Billy Bremner finds Johnny Giles on the left and his threaded pass to Mick Jones sees the hard-working striker cross into the six-yard box, where Peter Lorimer's touch takes him past his marker before he thumps it home from a couple of yards out.

19 March 1975
Anderlecht v Leeds United, European Cup quarter-final, second leg

Billy Bremner confirms the inevitable as he scores the only goal of the second leg to book a semi-final spot for United. Already 3-0 down from the first leg, the Belgians give as good as they get in an attempt to turn the tie around, but on a night when torrential rain falls and makes the pitch no more than a mud bath, the Whites put the hosts out of their misery with a superb goal. Peter Lorimer skips past a challenge on the left before looking up and spotting Bremner on the edge of the box. His deep cross looks set to be headed clear, but the defender misjudges the flight, whereas Bremner never takes his eye off it, chests the ball down and as the keeper races off his line he impudently dinks it over his head and into the net to secure a 1-0 victory and a 4-0 aggregate win for Jimmy Armfield's side. A wonderful piece of skill by one of United's greatest-ever players.

23 October 2020
Aston Villa v Leeds United, Premier League

Patrick Bamford completes a remarkable 22-minute hat-trick at Villa Park as the Whites go 3-0 up. It is a fine team move that starts with the keeper and ends with Hélder Costa playing a one-two with Jamie Shackleton before feeding Bamford ten yards from goal. There are three Villa players around him, but crucially none makes a challenge or closes him down, so after teeing himself up, Bamford opts to curl a shot past his markers and inside the left-hand post for a superb strike, his third of the evening. It will seal a fine 3-0 victory for Marcelo Bielsa's fearless side.

75

28 April 1962
Newcastle United v Leeds United, Second Division

Leeds fans inside St James' Park can finally start to relax as the Whites go 3-0 up. Needing just a point to send Bristol Rovers to the third tier, Don Revie's side seal victory over a Newcastle side with little but pride to play for, when promising youngster Billy Bremner's centre is inadvertently turned past his own keeper by Newcastle right-back Bobby Keith.

24 September 2003
Leeds United v Swindon Town, League Cup second round

The Whites look to be heading out of the League Cup at the first time of asking as third-tier Swindon lead 2-0 at Elland Road. To make matters worse, the Robins have been reduced to ten men and Peter Reid's side are set for an embarrassing loss – unless United can produce something special. Hopes rise when Aaron Lennon's corner is nodded on towards the edge of the box, where Ian Harte volleys a low shot home to halve the deficit.

19 July 2020
Derby County v Leeds United, Championship

Champions Leeds go 2-1 up away to Derby with a move that slices the Rams' defence apart. When Tyler Roberts receives the ball midway inside the Derby half, there seems little obvious danger for the hosts, but Roberts does a neat turn and then threads a pass through for Jamie Shackleton, who buries a low shot past the keeper and into the bottom-left corner to make it 2-1.

76

4 November 2000
Leeds United v Liverpool, Premier League

Mark Viduka's fourth goal of the game is enough to seal a thrilling 4-3 win over Liverpool, who had twice led at Elland Road. And there is an element of déjà vu about United's fourth as Olivier Dacourt drills a low pass into Viduka's feet and the Aussie striker uses his pace to spin off his marker and, as keeper Sander Westerveld races off his line, Viduka deftly chips the ball over his head – just as he had with the opening Leeds goal – to put the Whites ahead for the first time in this Premier League classic.

5 April 2003
Charlton Athletic v Leeds United, Premier League

Harry Kewell completes a memorable afternoon in south London as United's hopes of avoiding the drop receive a huge boost. The Whites had lost their previous six games and seen manager Terry Venables sacked as they fell towards the Premier League relegation zone, but the arrival of caretaker boss Peter Reid sees a sparkling performance that turns the form book upside down. Kewell is quick to intercept a poor pass before lashing a left-foot shot past the keeper to make it 6-1.

77

28 May 1971
Juventus v Leeds United, Inter-Cities Fairs Cup Final, first leg

Mick Bates grabs a crucial second away goal for Leeds in Turin. With the hosts 2-1 up and looking for a third, United launch a swift counter-attack that sees Johnny Giles send in a cross from the left and Massimo Piloni's attempted clearance falls for Bates, who hammers a shot that the Juve keeper can only push into the roof of the net. It's only Bates's second touch of the game having just come on as a sub, and the goal means Don Revie's men secure a 2-2 first leg away draw.

26 April 1992
Sheffield United v Leeds United, First Division

The most crucial goal of Leeds' First Division championship race comes via the head of a Sheffield United player. A long clearance upfield is headed on by Eric Cantona and into the path of Rod Wallace, but a Blades defender gets there first and knocks the ball back towards his own goal. As it bounces, Mel Rees runs out and Brian Gayle knees it in the air and then heads it over the keeper under pressure from Cantona and Wallace and into the empty net to put the Whites 3-2 up. It caps a comical afternoon of defending by the Blades and gives Leeds the three points. Manchester United's defeat by Liverpool later that Sunday afternoon guarantees Leeds a first top-flight title for 18 years.

8 August 1992
Leeds United v Liverpool, FA Charity Shield

Eric Cantona restores Leeds' advantage against Liverpool. As a free kick is floated into the Reds' box, Cantona rises to knock the ball down to Rod Wallace, who manages to return the favour to the enigmatic French star, who lashes it past Bruce Grobbelaar from eight yards to make it 3-2.

19 November 2005
Southampton v Leeds United, Championship

Southampton's nerves jangle yet further as United pull another goal back at St Mary's. Sub David Healy, who had won the corner that had led to the first goal, is again instrumental as he gets into the Saints' box and squares the ball to Robbie Blake, who drills hard and low past the keeper to make it 3-2 with 13 minutes still to play.

16 December 2020
Leeds United v Newcastle United, Premier League

United regain the lead in an entertaining clash with Newcastle at Elland Road. The visitors look to be in control in defence but overplay instead of clearing the Leeds press and give the ball away. Patrick Bamford feeds Mateusz Klich on the left and his dinked cross into the middle picks out Stuart Dallas at the far post to give the Whites a 3-2 advantage with just 13 minutes remaining.

78

3 March 1972
Leeds United v Southampton, First Division

Leeds complete a magnificent afternoon with a seventh goal against punch-drunk Southampton. In reality, it could and probably should have ended in a double-figure win for the Whites, but Don Revie's men score no more after Eddie Gray skips past a challenge on the left and picks out Peter Lorimer in the penalty area, where he heads back across the six-yard box and Mick Jones makes no mistake from close range.

9 May 1973
Leeds United v Arsenal, First Division

United continue to take an incredibly frustrating end to the 1972/73 campaign out on Arsenal. Billy Bremner makes it 4-1 against the second-placed Gunners at Elland Road as Don Revie's side prove that, at their best, few teams in England or overseas can live with them. Bremner's superb backwards header from a teasing Johnny Giles cross wraps up victory, though the Whites are far from finished with the Londoners.

9 April 1975
Leeds United v Barcelona, European Cup semi-final, first leg

Having seen Barcelona score a crucial away goal to make it 1-1 just 12 minutes before, the urgency to get a second for Leeds is palpable. The inspirational Johan Cruyff is threatening to give the Catalans a victory to take back to Spain, but Paul Reaney sends in a cross towards the back post, where the excellent Joe Jordan stretches to head back into the middle and, though Terry Yorath's overhead attempt fails, he does enough to distract his marker and the ball falls to Allan Clarke who buries a shot into the net from six yards to seal a 2-1 first-leg lead.

14 August 2007
Macclesfield Town v Leeds United, League Cup first round

United finally get the breakthrough against their League Two hosts, who had battled hard throughout, but 12 minutes from time, the Whites grab what will be the only goal of the game as David Prutton picks out Ian Westlake in the box to drill home a fine volley and secure victory for Dennis Wise's side.

29 November 2009
Kettering Town v Leeds United, FA Cup second round

Jermaine Beckford's late equaliser spares United's blushes as Kettering Town had threatened to become the second non-league side in successive years to dump the Whites out of the competition. The hosts had gone ahead at Rockingham Road through Ian Roper's goal just past the hour, but Beckford earns a replay as he diverts Robert Snodgrass's low cross past keeper Lee Harper – with a trip to face Manchester United at Old Trafford the carrot for the winners.

29 April 2017
Leeds United v Norwich City, Championship

United complete a dramatic comeback from 3-0 down to level at 3-3 against Norwich, and with enough time to search for what had looked an unlikely victory. Pablo Hernández curls a fine free kick over the wall and past the keeper for the equaliser in a game Leeds must win to keep their slender hopes of making the play-offs alive. But despite the stirring fightback and the visitors then having a man sent off, Garry Monk's side can't find a winner in the time that remains.

79

23 May 2021
Leeds United v West Bromwich Albion, Premier League

With his 17th Premier League goal of the season, it is fitting that Patrick Bamford is Leeds' last scorer in 2020/21. As a cross comes in from the left, Okay Yokuşlu stretches out an arm in a bid to hoodwink the referee into thinking that the ball had hit his chest, but the ref has spotted it and points to the spot. Bamford sends keeper Sam Johnstone the wrong way to make it 3-0 and, despite a late consolation for the visitors, Leeds confirm a top-ten finish and record the most points for a promoted side since Ipswich Town in 2000/01.

80

7 October 1967
Leeds United v Chelsea, First Division

Leeds hit a sixth against a woeful Chelsea at Elland Road with a goal that sums up the visitors' ineptitude. Having shipped five goals in the opening hour, the only surprise is perhaps how Chelsea manage to keep out another for 20 minutes but it arrives when Peter Lorimer's corner is headed into his own net by Marvin Hinton.

9 May 1973
Leeds United v Arsenal, First Division

It is two goals in three minutes for rampant Leeds who go 5-1 up against the team who had finished as the second best in the country. Terry Yorath's driving run forward sees the Welsh star find Mick Jones, who in turn feeds the hard-working Joe Jordan who makes no mistake with a drive past Bob Wilson.

12 September 1995
AS Monaco v Leeds United, UEFA Cup first round, first leg

Tony Yeboah completes his hat-trick as he chases a through ball and then knocks it over keeper Marc Delaroche, who gets a glove on the ball but can't stop it going over his head and into the back of the net. The goal puts United 3-0 up against the French side and makes it 20 in 23 appearances for the Ghanaian striker – but a sickening clash of heads between Delaroche and defender Basile

Boli, who had been chasing back with Yeboah, ends with emergency medical attention with both players who are seemingly out cold. Neither can continue and worrying TV pictures confirm the seriousness of the collision.

5 December 2000
Lazio v Leeds United, Champions League second group stage

Leeds snatch a superb away victory in Rome. Having lost their opening game at home to Real Madrid, United knew that a second defeat would likely scupper hopes of progressing out of a particularly difficult group, but it turns out to be an excellent and mature display by David O'Leary's men. The only goal of the game against Sven-Göran Eriksson's Lazio comes ten minutes from the end when Harry Kewell plays a pass to Alan Smith, who then feeds the ball into the feet of Mark Viduka. The Australian returns the favour with a brilliant back-heel that leaves Smith with just the keeper to beat and the youngster makes no mistake, tucking a low shot into the bottom-right corner to give the Whites a famous 1-0 win.

13 May 2001
Leeds United v Bradford City, Premier League

Bradford's aim to at least get a 0-0 draw in the second half after being savaged 5-1 in the first ends when United finally get a sixth ten minutes from time. Ian Harte's cross lands between a defender and Lee Bowyer, but falls more kindly for the United midfielder who then sweeps home from six yards.

17 August 2002
Leeds United v Manchester City, Premier League

Republic of Ireland striker Robbie Keane climbs off the bench to score the third goal of a 3-0 victory over newly promoted Manchester City at a packed Elland Road. City's poor defending continues as Keane finds space in the box and then sends an excellent lob over Carlo Nash to put the icing on a fine opening-day victory as Terry Venables gets one over on his fellow former England boss Kevin Keegan.

9 February 2010
Carlisle United v Leeds United, Football League Trophy northern area final, second leg

Having gone behind again and trailing 2-1 to Carlisle United on the day and 4-2 on aggregate, Leeds' chances of making the Wembley final against Southampton look unlikely at best – but Jason Crowe's equaliser ten minutes from time changes everything as he plants Gary McSheffrey's cross into the top-left corner from 12 yards out to make it 2-2 and leave the Whites needing one goal more to force a penalty shoot-out.

19 September 2017
Burnley v Leeds United, League Cup third round

In what will be a frantic end to the game at Turf Moor, Hadi Sacko gives United a 1-0 lead. Sub Pablo Hernández creates the goal with a burst forward and cross that Sacko converts to put the Whites seemingly on the way to victory in Lancashire.

81

9 May 1973
Leeds United v Arsenal, First Division

Leeds fans are left wondering what might have been as Joe Jordan grabs his second in two minutes – and United's third in four minutes – to make it 6-1 at Elland Road. Jordan rises to nod Peter Lorimer's cross past Bob Wilson to complete the scoring and end the 1972/73 league campaign in style, though few supporters are in any doubt that it could and should have been so much more as the Whites yet again missed out on glory with poor form in the final furlong.

22 February 1995
Leeds United v Everton, Premier League

Tony Yeboah grabs his first Premier League goal since joining from Eintracht Frankfurt in a deal worth £3.4m a few weeks previously. It will be enough to win the game 1-0 and is the start of an explosive spell with the Whites that will yield 32 goals in 66 starts, before injuries hamper his career in Yorkshire and he moves back to Germany.

21 February 2001
Anderlecht v Leeds United, Champions League second group stage

Leeds complete a 4-1 victory away to Anderlecht with an Ian Harte penalty rounding off a superb display. It will be a win that puts United in the quarter-finals at the very first attempt and the icing on the cake comes when Mark Viduka is felled by Glen De Boeck in the box and Harte coolly strokes the ball home to send the travelling United fans home dreaming of European glory.

27 August 2019
Leeds United v Stoke City, League Cup second round

Hélder Costa levels to ultimately earn a penalty shoot-out against Stoke City. The Whites, playing in front of a crowd of more than 30,000 at Elland Road, equalise when Leif Davis's fine cross from the left is headed home by Costa in the six-yard box to square up the tie at 2-2.

82

7 October 1967
Leeds United v Chelsea, First Division

It's seventh heaven for Don Revie's Leeds as Chelsea's capitulation at Elland Road is complete – and the goal that makes it 7-0 against the managerless visitors is easily the best of the lot as Billy Bremner spectacularly sends a Brazilian-style overhead kick past Peter Bonetti to the delight of a packed home crowd. It also sets a Football League record as the first time a team had registered seven different scorers in one game.

1 December 2018
Sheffield United v Leeds United, Championship

Pablo Hernández scores a vital late winner away to promotion rivals Sheffield United to strengthen the Whites' hopes of going up. The Blades are architects of their own downfall as Dean Henderson chases John Egan's overhit back pass to avoid conceding a corner, but while the on-loan Manchester United keeper does that, his miscued pass out goes straight to Jack Clarke who then tees up Hernández to tap home the only goal of the game and send 3,000 Leeds fans delirious.

83

12 April 1987
Coventry City v Leeds United, FA Cup semi-final

Keith Edwards keeps Leeds' FA Cup dreams alive as he makes it 2-2 against Coventry at Hillsborough. With the Sky Blues coming from behind to lead 2-1 as the clock ticked down, the Whites conjure up an equaliser as Andy Ritchie holds off one challenge on the right of the penalty area, then another, before floating a cross towards the six-yard box, where the predatory Edwards arrives on cue to power home past Steve Ogrizovic and send the game into extra time.

14 November 2002
Hapoel Tel Aviv v Leeds United, UEFA Cup second round, second leg

A dream evening for Alan Smith is complete as he scores his fourth of the evening to wrap up a 4-1 win over Hapoel Tel Aviv. Smith's incredible feat is secured as Harry Kewell sends in a another superb cross that the forward barely has to strain his neck muscles to nod home his and Leeds fourth of a memorable night in the Israeli capital.

84

20 April 1970
Chelsea v Leeds United, FA Cup Final

Late drama comes at Wembley in a pulsating final between Chelsea and Leeds. With the scores level at 1-1 and the clock ticking towards full time, both sides had gone close to scoring a second. When Eddie Gray crashes a shot off the crossbar, it looks as though Don Revie's men may need to go to extra time to try and win the game – until a fine ball from Billy Bremner sends Johnny Giles galloping down the right and his cross is headed against the post by Allan Clarke, but the rebound finds its way to Mick Jones, who drills a low shot into the bottom-left corner of the net. With just six minutes remaining, it looks like United's long wait for the FA Cup might finally be over, but Chelsea will level just two minutes later to force extra time and eventually a replay at Old Trafford.

19 November 2005
Southampton v Leeds United, Championship

United's remarkable fightback gets even better when Danny Higginbotham is penalised for handball in the box and the referee points to the spot. Super sub David Healy, who had already had a hand in two goals, steps up to power the penalty into the top-left corner to make it 3-3 with time still to cap off what would be an incredible comeback.

29 December 2019
Birmingham City v Leeds United, Championship

In an incredible game at St Andrew's, United score the seventh goal of a thoroughly entertaining contest to make it 4-3. The Blues had fought back from 2-0 down and 3-2 down to level twice, but when Luke Ayling finds Stuart Dallas in the box, he hooks the ball past the keeper to seemingly give the Whites three points – but there are more twists and turns to come in this incredible game.

31 January 2021
Leicester City v Leeds United, Premier League

United's counter-attacking football is just too good for Leicester as the Whites go 3-1 up at the King Power Stadium. A razor-sharp break down the left wing sees Mateusz Klich send Patrick Bamford clear in the Foxes' half and, as he reaches the box, he squares it to his right for Jack Harrison to finish the move with a low shot past Kasper Schmeichel to wrap up the win.

8 May 2021
Leeds United v Tottenham Hotspur, Premier League

Leeds secure a fine victory over Spurs by going 3-1 up with just six minutes of regulation time remaining. Raphinha looks well offside as he is played clear on the left flank, but the Brazilian does the right thing by powering towards the box and, with Spurs' defenders slow to get back in position, Raphinha's ball makes it easy for Rodrigo to slot home from eight yards.

19 July 2020
Derby County v Leeds United, Championship

Champions United wrap up a 3-1 win away to Derby. Ezgjan Alioski curls an out-swinging ball into the Rams' six-yard box and defender Matt Clarke tries to guide it behind for a corner but gets his clearance horribly wrong as he gently slices the ball past his own goalkeeper.

85

11 May 1999
Leeds United v Arsenal, Premier League

Leeds snatch a late victory to virtually hand the Premier League title to Manchester United. The Gunners, in the box seat to retain the championship, couldn't afford to lose at Elland Road with the Red Devils neck and neck with them at the top of the table and two games remaining – but with just five minutes left, Leeds, who had earlier missed a penalty, finally get the breakthrough as Harry Kewell jinks past Lee Dixon on the left of the box before crossing to the back post where Jimmy Floyd Hasselbaink dives to head past David Seaman and give the Whites a dramatic 1-0 victory.

16 December 2020
Leeds United v Newcastle United, Premier League

Breathing space at last for Marcelo Bielsa's men who go 4-2 up against Newcastle United at Elland Road. The Whites swiftly counter-attack down the middle through Raphinha who leads the charge forward. The Brazilian is soon joined by four of his team-mates to outnumber the Magpies five to two, so he plays the ball to his right for Pablo Hernández, who immediately squares it to one of his three unmarked team-mates inside the box, and Ezgjan Alioski takes a touch before lifting a shot over the keeper to put the hosts in firm control in the dying minutes.

86

25 February
Leeds United v Birmingham City, League Cup semi-final, second leg

Game, set and match for the Whites who complete a 3-0 win over Birmingham City at Elland Road and, with a 5-1 aggregate advantage, book a place in the League Cup Final against Aston Villa. The third goal comes when Rod Wallace works the ball out to Gary McAllister on the left flank. McAllister gets it under control before sending a cross towards the back post, where Brian Deane nods home to complete a comfortable victory for Howard Wilkinson's men.

19 November 2005
Southampton v Leeds United, Championship

Perhaps one of United's greatest-ever comebacks is complete as Liam Miller drills home the winner from eight yards out. Having been 3-0 down just 15 minutes earlier, a David Healy-inspired fightback had seen the Whites swarm over the Saints and score three times to make it 3-3. But the men in white were far from finished and the winner comes as Rob Hulse spots Miller – on loan from Manchester United – around the penalty spot, crosses in low and Miller's shot wrong-foots Saints keeper Antti Niemi and nestles in the back of the net, sending the 4,000 travelling Leeds fans into ecstasy at St Mary's.

9 February 2010
Carlisle United v Leeds United, Football League Trophy northern area final, second leg

The travelling thousands from Yorkshire go wild as Mike Grella scores the goal that finally levels the aggregate against Carlisle at Brunton Park. The hosts had twice led to bolster their 2-1 first-leg advantage, but the Whites refuse to throw the towel in and, when Gary McSheffrey's left-wing cross comes in, Grella plants a low drive into the bottom-left corner to make it 3-2 to Leeds and 4-4 on aggregate. The goal forces the game to a penalty shoot-out.

87

8 August 1992
Leeds United v Liverpool, FA Charity Shield

When a clearance appears to be going out for a Leeds corner, Rod Wallace is more alert than anyone as it hits the flag and bounces back towards him. At first glance, it looks as though Wallace had taken the corner to himself, but by the time the Liverpool defence realises what has happened, the forward has crossed into the middle and Eric Cantona leaps higher than anyone else to nod home for his hat-trick and put the Whites 4-2 up at Wembley.

28 December 2009
Stockport County v Leeds United, League One

Having trailed 2-1 to the bottom team, United get their noses back in front when it matters most in the dying minutes. A ball into the County box eventually finds its way out to Leigh Bromby and he lashes a low, right foot shot into the bottom-left corner to put league leaders United 3-2 up at Edgeley Park.

88

9 January 2000
Manchester City v Leeds United, FA Cup third round

Leeds wrap up a 5-2 victory away to Manchester City to progress to the fourth round of the FA Cup. Second-tier City had twice led and given as good as they got, but David O'Leary's side's greater class eventually won the day and a burst down the left by Darren Huckerby and cut-back to Harry Kewell sees the Australian tap home and wrap up a fine performance by the Whites in Moss Side.

4 May 2003
Arsenal v Leeds United, Premier League

A bittersweet moment on so many levels as Dominic Matteo drives forward having witnessed Arsenal strike the foot of the post moments before and his lofted pass sees Mark Viduka spin back onside and then head towards goal. Viduka cuts inside one challenge and then curls a beauty past David Seaman to give the Whites a 3-2 win that ensures top-flight safety, but also ends the Gunners' title hopes and gifts the Premier League crown to Manchester United.

16 December 2020
Leeds United v Newcastle United, Premier League

United seal three points against Newcastle with a stunning fifth of the evening. Having been punished on the break three minutes earlier, Steve Bruce's side haven't learned their lesson and Pablo Hernández plays a low ball out of defence to Jack Harrison, who drives towards the Magpies box alone. With three defenders around him, Harrison nudges it left before unleashing a 25-yard shot into the top-right corner of the net to make it 5-2 and seal a fine win with the goal of the night. Hernández's two assists also make him the oldest Leeds player to set up two top-flight goals in the same game since Gordon Strachan in 1993.

89

31 March 1965
Leeds United v Manchester United, FA Cup semi-final replay

Billy Bremner grabs a dramatic last-minute winner against Manchester United at Nottingham Forest's City Ground to send Leeds to their first FA Cup Final. With time ticking towards the 90-minute mark, a free kick is awarded on the halfway line; it's a chance to seal victory. Johnny Giles pumps the ball to the left of the six-yard box, where Bremner superbly guides it past the Manchester United keeper to make it 1-0 and send the Whites to Wembley where Liverpool await in the final. It's a superb goal by the little Scot who is immediately mobbed by his team-mates.

26 April 1971
Leeds United v Arsenal, First Division

Needing a victory to overhaul Arsenal at the top of the table and keep the title race alive, United grab a last-gasp winner at Elland Road. Paul Madeley wins possession of the ball and plays the ball to Allan Clarke just inside the Gunners' box. Clarke prods a shot towards the goal and Jack Charlton. As keeper Bob Wilson races out, Charlton squeezes the ball past him and sees his shot strike the post before hitting an Arsenal player and rolling into the back of the net. Despite vehement appeals for offside by the Arsenal players, the goal stands and gives the Whites a 1-0 victory – but the north London side have games in hand, which they win, to deny Don Revie's side glory.

5 March 1975
Leeds United v Anderlecht, European Cup quarter-final, first leg

United grab a crucial third first-leg goal to leave Anderlecht with a mountain to climb in the return game. With the clock ticking towards 90 minutes and the outplayed Belgians hoping to get away with just a two-goal loss on a foggy evening at Elland Road, the Whites launch one final attack to try and get the job done on home soil. The influential Eddie Gray sees a shot blocked, but Peter Lorimer follows up to thunder home the loose ball from 12 yards to make it 3-0 and make the second leg that much more comfortable.

14 May 1987
Leeds United v Oldham Athletic, Second Division play-off semi-final, first leg

The prolific Keith Edwards, signed from neighbours Sheffield United, grabs a dramatic late winner to give the Whites a 1-0 victory over Oldham Athletic and a narrow lead to take to Boundary Park in the second leg. Billy Bremner's side had been knocking on the door throughout the second half and a set piece finally ends the Latics' resistance as John Sheridan's free kick from the right is nodded home by Edwards at the near post to send Elland Road wild.

27 February 1996
Port Vale v Leeds United, FA Cup fifth round replay

With extra time beckoning at Vale Park, a late challenge on Carlton Palmer gives United a chance to win the game inside 90 minutes. A home quarter-final against Liverpool, the reward for the winners, means there is plenty at stake as Gary McAllister and Tony Yeboah stand by the ball some 20 yards out. Yeboah runs forward but steps over it and McAllister pauses, sizing up the Vale goal before curling a sumptuous free kick into the top-right corner to make it 2-1 and win the game for the Whites.

19 September 2000
Leeds United v AC Milan, Champions League first group stage

Lee Bowyer grabs a crucial late winner against AC Milan to boost United's confidence in the Champions League following an opening group stage thrashing by Barcelona in Spain. Though injury-hit, the Whites turn in a spirited display and look set to record a creditable 0-0 draw until the Italian side's keeper Dida makes a huge error to hand David O'Leary's men a 1-0 victory. Lee Bowyer opts for a hopeful 30-yard shot in the dying embers of normal time and Dida gets it all wrong as he attempts to beat the ball down and then watches in horror as the momentum carries the shot over the line to the delight of the Elland Road crowd.

10 August 2016
Fleetwood Town v Leeds United, League Cup first round

Trailing to a 13th-minute goal, United leave it late to force extra time with a scrambled equaliser at Highbury. As a move down the left progresses, the ball finds its way into the box and eventually to the feet of Marcus Antonsson who swivels and fires home from close range to make it 1-1.

90

17 September 1969
Leeds United v Lyn, European Cup first round, first leg

Billy Bremner's late strike means United hit double figures on their European Cup debut. Ironically, the 25 minutes that had passed were the most Lyn had managed without conceding in the game, but when Bremner is allowed all the time in the world to tee himself up on the edge of the box he accepts the opportunity and his shot from 20 yards beats the keeper via a deflection to complete the rout.

16 May 1973
Leeds United v AC Milan, European Cup Winners' Cup Final

To seal a miserable night in Greece, Norman Hunter is sent off in the last minute against AC Milan. Rarely has a game involving the Whites been subject to such poor officiating, with the Greek referee denying Leeds two penalties and seemingly favouring AC Milan on numerous borderline decisions. Even the Greek fans in the largely neutral crowd were booing the referee and Milan players because of the perceived injustice. When Hunter's burst forward is subjected to another cynical hack down the calf, the Leeds defender goes looking for revenge and floors Gianni Rivera before being sent off for the offence. The Italians hold on to win 1-0.

17 May 1987
Oldham Athletic v Leeds United, Second Division play-off semi-final, second leg

Keith Edwards is once again the scourge of Oldham as he pops up to secure a place in the play-off final against Charlton. Edwards's 89th-minute header had settled the first leg at Elland Road and he is the last-gasp hero again as Leeds score with almost the final kick of the second leg at Boundary Park. It is all the more dramatic as Oldham had just gone 2-0 up on 89 minutes to seemingly win the tie, but Edwards coolly slots home in the dying seconds after Neil Aspin's cross is headed into his path by John Pearson to make it 2-1 and force extra time – and with no further scoring, the Whites win on away goals.

13 October 1999
Leeds United v Blackburn Rovers, League Cup third round

United snatch victory with almost the last kick of the game to send Blackburn Rovers crashing out at Elland Road. When Darren Huckerby is fouled by Craig Short on the edge of the box, it gives Danny Mills the chance to have a crack at goal – and the full-back doesn't disappoint as he drills home what proves to be the only goal of the game and his second of the season.

28 October 1995
Leeds United v Coventry City, Premier League

Gary McAllister strokes home the penalty that completes his hat-trick against Coventry. The Scotland midfielder had bagged two in the first half and he finally sees the Sky

Blues off, tucking the ball into the bottom-left corner to ensure he leaves Elland Road with the match ball.

24 September 2003
Leeds United v Swindon Town, League Cup second round

An 'I was there' moment as United grab a last-gasp equaliser against League One Swindon Town to stay in the League Cup. The ten-man visitors had gone 2-0 up and had just 15 minutes to see out when Ian Harte pulled a goal back. But with just seconds of the 90 left, United win a corner and goalkeeper Paul Robinson comes up to join the attack. The first corner is cleared out for another flag-kick and with it being a last throw of the dice, Robinson stays up. This time, a short corner is rolled to Michael Bridges – playing his first game for eight months – and the second-half sub whips in a cross to the edge of the six-yard box, where Robinson meets it perfectly to glance a header into the far corner to send a near-30,000 Elland Road crowd crazy. It is a goal that any number nine would be proud of and it forces extra time.

90+1

10 April 2021
Manchester City v Leeds United, Premier League

Ten-man Leeds stun champions-elect Manchester City with an added-time winner at the Etihad Stadium. United had defended their 1-0 lead until the 75th minute when Ferran Torres levelled for the hosts, who had gone into the game some 32 points ahead of Marcelo Bielsa's side. But in a dramatic twist, Ezgjan Alioski splits the home defence with a threaded ball into Stuart Dallas's path and the Leeds man bags his second goal of the game with a low shot through Ederson's legs to secure a fine 2-1 victory over Pep Guardiola's team. It also means that Leeds, in their first season back in the Premier League, have taken four points off the side who will soon be comfortably crowned Premier League champions.

15 May 2008
Carlisle United v Leeds United, League One play-off semi-final, second leg

Johnny Howson grabs the second goal to send Leeds to Wembley in a thrilling finish at Brunton Park. With the board going up to signal just one added minute to play and the tie balanced at 2-2 on aggregate, the Whites launch one final attack on the Carlisle defence and, as the ball is laid off by Dougie Freedman to Howson, the youngster works himself a yard of space on the edge of the box before drilling a low, left-foot shot into the bottom-right corner to make it 2-0 and send Gary McAllister's side to Wembley.

90+2

31 March 2001
Sunderland v Leeds United, Premier League

Ten-man Leeds secure victory over Sunderland at the Stadium of Light with an added-time goal from Mark Viduka. A quick free kick just inside the Black Cats' half catches the home side out before Robbie Keane collects and plays a cross into the box, where Viduka arrives to slide the ball past Thomas Sørensen and seal a 2-0 win.

19 October 2009
Leeds United v Norwich City, League One

Jermaine Beckford grabs a dramatic last-gasp winner as Leeds secure a 2-1 victory over Norwich. The League One promotion battle seems to be heading for a draw – one that the Canaries would have deserved – until an added-time howler by keeper Fraser Forster. As the ball comes to Forster, he badly scuffs his clearance to the feet of the lurking Beckford, who calmly slots it past the crestfallen stopper to give United three points and move Simon Grayson's men back to the top of the table.

90+3

28 December 2009
Stockport County v Leeds United, League One

Jermaine Beckford's second of the afternoon ensures that the points travel back over the Pennines with Leeds after a surprisingly tough afternoon against a Stockport side rooted to the foot of the table having lost their previous ten games. The goal that finally kills off plucky County comes when Trésor Kandol nods a long ball on into the path of Beckford, who runs on and lashes a low shot home from just inside the box to make it 4-2 and claim his 19th of the season. The victory keeps United eight points clear of second-placed Charlton and, crucially, 11 points clear of third-placed Norwich in the battle to escape the third tier.

9 July 2020
Leeds United v Stoke City, Championship

The ruthless Championship leaders complete a miserable day for visitors Stoke with a fully deserved fifth goal at a buoyant Elland Road. Luke Ayling is the creator, sending a 40-yard ball into the path of the excellent Patrick Bamford, who hits a low, left-foot drive across the keeper and into the bottom-right corner to edge Marcelo Bielsa's men ever closer to promotion.

16 September 2020
Leeds United v Hull City, League Cup second round

Ezgjan Alioski saves United's blushes against League One side Hull with an equaliser deep into added time.

Trailing after just five minutes to an early goal from the Tigers, it seems the Whites will exit the competition at the first hurdle until a scramble in the box sees Alioski fire a shot into the top-right corner of the net to force a penalty shoot-out with the Humberside outfit.

90+4

10 August 2016
Fleetwood Town v Leeds United, League Cup first round

Leeds take a stoppage-time lead against Fleetwood Town at Highbury. As the ball is played to Marcus Antonsson, who had managed to get behind the Fleetwood defence, he is brought down by a clumsy challenge and the referee awards a penalty. Chris Wood steps up to send the keeper the wrong way and put United 2-1 up on the Fylde Coast.

19 September 2017
Burnley v Leeds United, League Cup third round

Having seen a 1-0 lead cruelly wiped out in the final minute of normal time by former Leeds favourite Chris Wood, the Whites have the chance to snatch a dramatic win when the referee points to the spot as Kemar Roofe is pulled back in the box. Pablo Hernández converts to make it 2-1 and surely send United into round four – yet there is still just enough time for Burnley's Robbie Brady to level for the Clarets two minutes later and force extra time – and then penalties.

90+5

12 May 2008
Leeds United v Carlisle United, League One play-off semi-final, first leg

With an expectant Elland Road in stunned silence after their promotion dream appears to be in tatters as Carlisle lead 2-0, the Whites launch one final attack deep into injury time. A long diagonal free kick is launched into the Cumbrians' box and when it falls to the on-loan Dougie Freedman, he sweeps home a low shot through the keeper's legs to give Leeds a vital lifeline going into the second leg.

29 December 2019
Birmingham City v Leeds United, Championship

After Birmingham had scored in added time to equalise for the third time in the game, United fans could have been forgiven for thinking their side had dropped two vital points at St Andrew's. At 4-4, few would argue that the Blues hadn't done enough to earn a point, but the final twist comes when a Birmingham player scores the ninth goal of an absorbing contest – fortunately for the Whites, it is in his own goal as Wes Harding nods Luke Ayling's cross past his own keeper to give Marcelo Bielsa's men a dramatic 5-4 win and put them back on top of the table.

18 May 2021
Southampton v Leeds United, Premier League

Tyler Roberts seals a fine 2-0 win away to Southampton with almost the last kick of the game at St Mary's. Roberts is heavily involved in the counter-attack that leads to the goal, seeing his first shot well saved by Alex McCarthy. Patrick Bamford's effort is also beaten out, but only as far as Roberts who is composed and calm as he stops the ball at his feet before calmly passing it into the bottom-right corner to ensure Marcelo Bielsa's side leave the south coast with all three points.

90+6

23 January 2010
Tottenham Hotspur v Leeds United, FA Cup fourth round

Trailing 2-1 with just seconds remaining, United are awarded a penalty and the chance to take Tottenham back to Elland Road for a replay. Jermaine Beckford takes on Michael Dawson in the box and the Spurs defender's attempt to put the ball out for a corner is clumsy as he scythes down the United striker. Beckford steps up to take the spot-kick and confidently plants the ball in the top-right corner to make it 2-2.

90+11

9 February 2019
Middlesbrough v Leeds United, Championship

Kalvin Phillips scores 11 minutes into added time to deny Middlesbrough victory at the Riverside Stadium. Boro had led since the 47th minute, but after paramedics had tended to Leeds teenager Jack Clarke, who had felt unwell after coming off at half-time, a sizeable amount of additional time was needed and the Whites take full advantage as Phillips heads Liam Cooper's cross past Darren Randolph to earn the point that moves United ahead of Norwich, who slipped to second. It remains one of the club's latest regulation-time equalisers.

Extra time

98

25 August 2009
Leeds United v Watford, League Cup, second round

After battling out a 1-1 draw over 90 minutes, Leeds and Watford are forced into a further 30 minutes of action to decide who will progress to the League Cup second round. Marvin Sordell's late equaliser had cancelled out Robert Snodgrass's first-half goal, but the Scotland star then scores what will be the only goal of extra time to clinch a 2-1 win. Just like his first of the evening, Snodgrass fires a low shot into the bottom-left corner to send the majority of the near-15,000 Elland Road crowd home happy.

99

29 May 1987
Leeds United v Charlton Athletic, Second Division play-off final replay

With Leeds having beaten First Division Charlton Athletic 1-0 at Elland Road in the second leg to draw 1-1 on aggregate, a deciding third game was required to see if the Addicks retained their top-flight status or the Whites would be promoted from the second tier. At a neutral venue, Birmingham's St Andrew's, United fans made up about 80 per cent of the 15,841 gate and, after neither side could be separated during normal time, an extra 30 minutes were needed to settle the contest – where it looked like Leeds would edge the game after John Sheridan's superb 20-yard free kick curled into the top-right corner to break the deadlock. But two Peter Shirtliff goals on 113 and 117 minutes are enough to see Charlton recover to win 2-1 and leave United supporters wondering what might have been.

100

1 May 1965
Liverpool v Leeds United, FA Cup Final

After an exhausting 0-0 draw in normal time, Billy Bremner grabs a dramatic, extra-time equaliser against Liverpool as United seek a first FA Cup triumph at Wembley. Having fallen behind to Roger Hunt's 93rd-minute goal, the Whites – who will agonisingly finish First Division runners-up to Manchester United on goal average on their return to the top flight this season – level in spectacular fashion as Jack Charlton rises to nod the ball down to Scottish legend Bremner who hits a first-time half-volley into the top-right corner from ten yards to send half of Wembley wild. Sadly, it doesn't set up the grandstand finish the Leeds fans were hoping for as Liverpool score seven minutes from the end of extra time to win the game 2-1.

108

8 December 2009

Leeds United v Kettering Town, FA Cup second round replay

United finally go back in front against a tiring Kettering Town to begin an astonishing four-goal burst in the second period of extra time. The goal comes after the persistence of Leigh Bromby on the right, who wriggles through several challenges before squeezing a low cross for Mike Grella to dispatch a rising, angled shot into the left of the goal to give the keeper no chance and put Leeds 2-1 up.

109

8 December 2009
Leeds United v Kettering Town, FA Cup second round replay

After keeping United out for the first 18 minutes of extra time, Kettering concede a second goal in the space of a minute to go 3-1 down. The non-league side had defended stoically for so long, but their resistance is well and truly ended as Robert Snodgrass clips an excellent cross to the far post for Trésor Kandol to head home from a couple of yards out and end the tie as a contest against the tiring part-timers.

25 October 2016
Leeds United v Norwich City, League Cup fourth round

United level against Norwich for the second time in an entertaining last-16 tie at Elland Road. In front of a crowd of 22,222, Chris Wood taps home Hadi Sacko's low cross from the right to make it 2-2 and with no further scoring on the night the game goes to penalties.

114

28 October 2003

Leeds United v Manchester United, League Cup third round

With the clock ticking towards the end of extra time, Elland Road erupts as the Whites draw level with Manchester United. In an action-packed match, the equaliser comes when James Milner's low cross from the right is bundled home by Roque Júnior – his second of the game – to make it 2-2. It will be the Red Devils who snatch a late winner to progress to the next round, however.

116

17 January 2006
Leeds United v Wigan Athletic, FA Cup third round replay

Gary Kelly is the unlikely hero deep into extra time as he makes it 3-3 with his first goal in three years. Wigan had led three times in the game, but each time the Whites fought back to level. However, with just minutes left, it seems as though the Latics' third will be enough to settle the tie until Kelly's wonder strike forces a penalty shoot-out. All three United goals come after corner kicks and, on this occasion, the ball is cleared out of the Wigan box to the lurking Kelly who chests the ball to his right before unleashing a volley from 25 yards out that flies into the right-hand corner to send Elland Road wild. To say the goal was somewhat unexpected from the Republic of Ireland international would be an understatement.

8 December 2009
Leeds United v Kettering Town, FA Cup second round replay

A superb goal from Mike Grella puts the Whites 4-1 up and confirms a third-round trip to face Manchester United. Grella, who had given Leeds the lead in the second half of extra time, carries the ball into the Kettering box before curling a sublime shot into the top-right corner. It is United's third goal in eight minutes and is perhaps a tad harsh on the non-league side, who have given as good as they have got.

119

8 December 2009
Leeds United v Kettering Town, FA Cup second round replay

Jermaine Beckford makes it four extra-time goals in the space of 12 blistering minutes as United wrap up a 5-1 win over Kettering. Mike Grella moves into the box on the right before slipping a pass to his left, where Trésor Kandol's low shot is turned in by Jermaine Beckford – who looked a shade offside – to complete a comprehensive win for the Whites.

Penalty shoot-outs

Some games run out of playing time and are forced to go to the dreaded penalty shoot-out. It's nail-biting and often unbearable to watch as well as being an emotional rollercoaster. Leeds United have had their fair share, both good and bad. Here is a selection of memorable (and not so memorable) shoot-outs.

10 August 1974
Liverpool v Leeds United, FA Charity Shield

One of the most bad-tempered FA Charity Shield matches of all time ends 1-1, and Liverpool and Leeds United are forced to decide the result from 12 yards.

- Peter Lorimer (Leeds United) scores – 0-1
- Alec Lindsay (Liverpool) scores – 1-1
- Johnny Giles (Leeds United) scores – 1-2
- Emlyn Hughes (Liverpool) scores – 2-2
- Eddie Gray (Leeds United) scores – 2-3
- Brian Hall (Liverpool) scores – 3-3
- Norman Hunter (Leeds United) scores – 3-4
- Tommy Smith (Liverpool) scores – 4-4
- Trevor Cherry (Leeds United) scores – 4-5
- Peter Cormack (Liverpool) scores – 5-5
- David Harvey (Leeds United) misses – 5-5
- Ian Callaghan (Liverpool) scores – 6-5

Liverpool win 6-5

29 September 1998
CS Marítimo v Leeds United, UEFA Cup first round, second leg

After Leeds won the first leg 1-0 at Elland Road, Portuguese side Marítimo won the return game 1-0 to make the overall aggregate score 1-1, forcing extra time and ultimately penalties.

- Alf-Inge Håland (Leeds United) scores – 1-0
- Alex Bunbury (CS Marítimo) scores – 1-1
- Ian Harte (Leeds United) scores – 2-1
- Paulo Sérgio (CS Marítimo) misses – 2-1
- Danny Granville (Leeds United) scores – 3-1
- Jorge Soares (CS Marítimo) misses – 3-1
- Lee Sharpe (Leeds United) scores – 4-1

Leeds United win 4-1

24 September 2003
Leeds United v Swindon Town, League Cup second round

Having come back from 2-0 down in the last 15 minutes against a side with ten men and from two divisions lower, United fail to see off the plucky Robins in extra time. Leeds keeper Paul Robinson had been the hero with a 90th-minute equaliser – but could he be the hero again in the shoot-out?

- Alan Smith (Leeds United) scores – 1-0
- Sam Parkin (Swindon Town) misses but the ball hits the post and then Paul Robinson for an own goal – 1-1
- Ian Harte (Leeds United) misses – 1-1
- Brian Howard (Swindon Town) scores – 1-2
- Michael Bridges (Leeds United) scores – 2-2
- Ian Herring (Swindon Town) scores – 2-3
- Roque Júnior (Leeds United) scores – 3-3
- Stefani Miglioranzi (Swindon Town) misses – 3-3
- Lucas Radebe (Leeds United) scores – 4-3
- Andy Gurney (Swindon Town) misses – 4-3

Leeds United win 4-3

17 January 2006
Leeds United v Wigan Athletic, FA Cup third round replay

After a thrilling 3-3 draw with Wigan Athletic, the teams cannot be separated and are forced into a penalty shoot-out.

- David Healy (Leeds United) misses – 0-0
- Jimmy Bullard (Wigan Athletic) scores – 0-1
- Richard Cresswell (Leeds United) scores – 1-1
- Gary Teale (Wigan Athletic) scores – 1-2
- Robbie Blake (Leeds United) scores – 2-2
- Jason Roberts (Wigan Athletic) scores – 2-3
- Rob Hulse (Leeds United) misses – 2-3
- Graham Kavanagh (Wigan Athletic) scores – 2-4

Wigan Athletic win 4-2

9 February 2010

Carlisle United v Leeds United, Football League Trophy northern area final, second leg

Leeds v Carlisle was an unlikely rivalry that raged for three years during which ten games were played, with both sides winning four times. This was the ninth of those encounters and was no less dramatic than those that went before. In this, the second leg of the Football League Trophy northern area final, Leeds had fought back from 4-2 down on aggregate to score twice in the last ten minutes. That set up a penalty shoot-out at Brunton Park for a place in the final at Wembley where Southampton awaited.

- Ian Harte (Carlisle United) scores – 1-0
- Bradley Johnson (Leeds United) misses – 1-0
- Kevan Hurst (Carlisle United) scores – 2-0
- Robert Snodgrass (Leeds United) scores – 2-1
- Gary Madine (Carlisle United) scores – 3-1
- Gary McSheffrey (Leeds United) scores – 3-2
- Richard Keogh (Carlisle United) misses – 3-2
- Mike Grella (Leeds United) scores – 3-3
- Adam Clayton (Carlisle United) scores – 4-3
- Max Gradel (Leeds United) scores – 4-4
- Evan Horwood (Carlisle United) scores – 5-4
- Neil Kilkenny (Leeds United) scores – 5-5
- Matt Robson (Carlisle United) scores – 6-5
- Shane Lowry (Leeds United) misses – 6-5

Carlisle United win 6-5

10 August 2016
Fleetwood Town v Leeds United, League Cup first round

With Leeds having trailed with a minute to go, then led during extra time, this topsy-turvy cup tie ends 2-2 and goes to a penalty shoot-out.

- Chris Wood (Leeds United) scores – 1-0
- Bobby Grant (Fleetwood Town) scores – 1-1
- Marcus Antonsson (Leeds United) scores – 2-1
- James Ryan (Fleetwood Town) scores – 2-2
- Alex Mowatt (Leeds United) scores 3-2
- Conor McLaughlin (Fleetwood Town) scores – 3-3
- Kalvin Phillips (Leeds United) scores – 4-3
- Ash Hunter (Fleetwood Town) scores – 4-4
- Pablo Hernández (Leeds United) scores – 5-4
- Eggert Jónsson (Fleetwood Town) – misses – 5-4

Leeds United win 5-4

25 October 2016
Leeds United v Norwich City, League Cup fourth round

Having twice come from behind, Leeds force a penalty shoot-out with Norwich City after a 2-2 draw at Elland Road as they go in search of a first quarter-final in 20 years

- Graham Dorrans (Norwich City) scores – 1-0
- Chris Wood (Leeds United) scores – 1-1
- Alex Pritchard (Norwich City) misses – 1-1
- Kemar Roofe (Leeds United) scores – 1-2
- Steven Naismith (Norwich City) misses – 1-2
- Kalvin Phillips (Leeds United) misses – 1-2
- Nélson Oliveira (Norwich City) scores – 2-2
- Matt Grimes (Leeds United) misses – 2-2
- Robbie Brady (Norwich City) misses – 2-2
- Ronaldo Vieira (Leeds United) scores – 2-3

Leeds United win 3-2

19 September 2017
Burnley v Leeds United, League Cup third round

After a frantic end to the game and four goals in 16 minutes, Leeds and Burnley must decide who goes into the last 16 with a penalty shoot-out at Turf Moor. The new 'ABBA' system of one penalty for one side followed by two each thereafter ensues.

- Pierre-Michel Lasogga (Leeds United) scores – 1-0
- Chris Wood (Burnley) scores – 1-1
- Ashley Barnes (Burnley) scores – 1-2
- Pablo Hernández (Leeds United) scores – 2-2
- Mateusz Klich (Leeds United) scores – 3-2
- Robbie Brady (Burnley) scores – 3-3
- James Tarkowski (Burnley) misses – 3-3
- Ezgjan Alioski (Leeds United) scores – 4-3
- Stuart Dallas (Leeds United) scores – 5-3

Leeds United win 5-3

27 August 2019
Leeds United v Stoke City, League Cup second round

United have come back from 2-0 down to force a shoot-out and go into it with the momentum of that recovery buoying the 30,000 Elland Road crowd.

- Sam Vokes (Stoke City) scores – 1-0
- Barry Douglas (Leeds United) scores – 1-1
- Mark Duffy (Stoke City) scores – 2-1
- Hélder Costa (Leeds United) scores – 2-2
- Peter Etebo (Stoke City) scores – 3-2
- Kalvin Phillips (Leeds United) scores – 3-3
- Sam Clucas (Stoke City) scores – 4-3
- Eddie Nketiah (Leeds United) scores – 4-4
- Jack Butland (Stoke City) scores – 5-4
- Jack Harrison (Leeds United) misses – 5-4

Stoke City win 5-4

16 September 2020
Leeds United v Hull City, League Cup second round

Having levelled with almost the last kick of the game to make it 1-1, United embark on a penalty shoot-out to decide who goes into the third round.

- Rodrigo (Leeds United) scores – 1-0
- Greg Docherty (Hull City) scores – 1-1
- Ezgjan Alioski (Leeds United) misses – 1-1
- Callum Jones (Hull City) scores – 1-2
- Tyler Roberts (Leeds United) scores – 2-2
- Lewie Coyle (Hull City) misses – 2-2
- Ian Poveda (Leeds United) scores – 3-2
- James Scott (Hull City) scores – 3-3
- Barry Douglas (Leeds United) scores – 4-3
- Thomas Mayer (Hull City) scores – 4-4
- Pascal Struijk (Leeds United) scores – 5-4
- Callum Elder (Hull City) scores – 5-5
- Leif Davis (Leeds United) scores – 6-5
- Sean McLoughlin (Hull City) scores – 6-6
- Robbie Gotts (Leeds United) scores – 7-6
- Billy Chadwick (Hull City) scores – 7-7
- Kiko Casilla (Leeds United) scores – 8-7
- Daniel Batty (Hull City) scores – 8-8
- Jamie Shackleton (Leeds United) misses – 8-8
- Alfie Jones (Hull City) scores – 8-9

Hull City win 9-8 on penalties

Also available at all good book stores

9781785316739

9781908051387

9781785315466

9781909178731

9781785315084

9781785317576

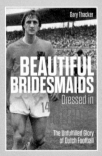

9781785318467

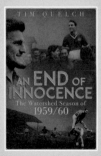

9781785317583

9781785315534